The Philosophy
of Consciousness
Without an Object

THE PHILOSOPHY OF CONSCIOUSNESS WITHOUT AN OBJECT

·

REFLECTIONS
ON THE NATURE OF
TRANSCENDENTAL CONSCIOUSNESS

Franklin Merrell-Wolff

Julian Press

Published by The Julian Press, Inc.,
a division of the Crown Publishing Group,
One Park Avenue, New York, New York 10016.
Published simultaneously in Canada by
General Publishing Company, Limited.

Manufactured in the United States of America

Library of Congress Cataloging in Publication Data
Merrell-Wolff, Franklin.
The philosophy of consciousness without an object;
reflections on the nature of transcendental consciousness.
New York, Julian Press, 1973
Includes bibliographical references.

1. Consciousness.   I. Title.

BF311.M448   126   73-82441 MARC

ISBN 0-517-52755-3 (cloth)
ISBN 0-517-54949-2 (paper)

10   9   8   7   6   5   4   3   2   1

1983 Edition

CONTENTS

PREFACE

●

While the present work presupposes acquaintance
with my earlier volume *Pathways Through to Space*,*
yet it may be read independently. The earlier contribution is a record of transformation in consciousness
written down during the actual process itself, and
thus, while it supplies a peculiarly intimate view, yet
it loses thereby something of the objective valuation
that only distance can contribute. In the present
volume a recapitulation of the record, written after
the fact, forms the material of the second chapter.

* New York: The Julian Press, Inc., 1973.

The perspective in this case is naturally more complete. As a result, the interpretative thought, which follows as the implication of the transformation, possesses a more explicit logical unity. The earlier writing was, of necessity, more in the form of a stream of ideas, composed as they welled up into the foreground of consciousness, rather than a systematic development. The writing was true to the thought of the day or the moment and synoptic in form in so far as it was related to the development of conceptions. Many problems were left incompletely handled, and this was done knowingly, with the intention subsequently to develop the thought more fully. The present book was planned to fill the gaps left in the earlier work.

However, despite my intention to write a logically organized system, I found, somewhat to my embarrassment, the thought persisted in growing in directions I had not foreseen. Formal systematic organization broke down again and again as the flow burst over the dams of preconceived structure. As a result, the present work is only somewhat more systematic than the *Pathways* but falls short of the requirements of a completed system. Clearly the time is not yet ripe for the rounding out of all parts. Some problems have received a clearer elucidation, but in the process others have arisen that remain unfinished.

He who knows the Awakening becomes something of a poet, no matter how little he was a poet before. No longer may thought remain purely formal. The poet pioneers, while the intellect systematizes. The one opens the Door, while the other organizes command. The functions are complementary. But in this combination there are difficulties as well as advantages. The thought that seeks the rounded system, which shall stand guarded on all sides, ever finds new Doors opening in unexpected places, and then, reorganization becomes necessary. The vistas appearing through each new Opening are far too valuable to be ignored, and besides, Truth cannot be honestly denied. So the system is never closed. I beg the critic to indulge this flaw, if flaw it is.

In the present volume I have found it even logically impossible to disregard the personal factor. By preference I would have written as Spinoza wrote, but in this day we are no longer free to disregard the epistemological problem. No longer can we take conceptions at their face value as carriers of Knowledge. Since the work of Kant we must ever question the authority of all conceptions. Always it is asked, what do the conceptions mean? And in general, they mean a somewhat which is not itself a conception. How, then, is the acquaintance with this somewhat, itself, attained? When the reference is to ordinary experience, the problem is simple enough and may often be assumed, but the Way of Consciousness that becomes available through the transformation is far from the beaten track, so it cannot be taken implicitly, if one would do the reader justice. For that reason a review of the process of transformation is introduced to provide the ground on which the more systematic discussion rests.

Today it is not necessary to prove that there are states of mystical consciousness possessing positive individual and social value. Too many writers of proven intellectual and scientific competency have given serious attention to the subject and have not only demonstrated the actuality of mystical states of consciousness but have found the results for feeling and character development excellent, at least in many instances. I can list the names of men like William James, John Dewey, Bertrand Russell, James H. Leuba, and Alexis Carrel, to say nothing of the great German Idealists who have either written directly from the awakened mystical sense, or at least, know full well its actuality. But with the exception of William James and the German Idealists, there is a general tendency among such students to claim that no true knowledge of reality, of the "thing-in-itself," can come from the mystical experience. As a result, the primary problem of the present work is the demonstration, as far as may be, of the actuality of noetic value springing from mystical or gnostic roots. I was forced, therefore, to give serious attention to philosophical and psychological criticism and to develop my thesis with an eye to the pitfalls indicated by such criticism. Much of this criticism is distinctly challenging and may not be lightly brushed aside. To him who has the poet's insight or the intuitive feeling of the unfettered religious nature, much of the critical part of the discussion will appear unnecessary and many modes of formulation unduly devious and recondite. To such I would say: "Be patient, and remember I am not writing only for those who believe easily. Know you not that there are men of intellectual power and honesty in this world who view you patronizingly as little, well-meaning, but credulous children? I would command for you respectful attention even though there may be much honest disagreement."

F.M.W.

PART I

The Ground
of Knowledge

Chapter 1

THE
IDEA
AND ITS
REFERENCE

●

The office of great philosophy is to be a *Way* of Realization, and not solely a monitor of *doing*. This the ancients knew well, but in these later, more sordid, days this truth is all but forgotten. The serious citizen of the present-day world may well blush when he thinks of what must be the judgment of the future historian who, when he writes of our age, notes how superb genius and skill served mainly the mundane needs and convenience of a "plantigrade, featherless, biped mammal of the genus homo" in its adaptations to environment, or else studied how very intricate and technical devices might be adapted to the destruction of that same mammal in the most unpleasant way conceivable. Indeed, when knowledge serves such ends, ignorance is preferable. But though it is ill enough when technical knowledge finds no more worthy objective, far worse and darker is it when the royal Queen of Knowledge is dragged down to the status of handmaiden of earthly science. Admittedly, by its very form and method, earthly science can find its ultimate justification only in doing, but it is the true office of philosophy to serve a more worthy and ultimate end. For the eternal function of the Divine Sophia is to supply the knowing that serves *being* first of all and *doing* only in so far as action is instrumental to that being.

The present sad estate of much philosophy is largely the result of a critical acumen that has run far ahead of the unfoldment of balancing insight. Far be it from me to question the valid functions of the critical spirit, for I would be among the last who would care to abide in a fool's castle of illusion; but criticism by itself leads only to the dead end of universal skepticism. To be sure, this skepticism may be variously disguised, as revealed in statements such as "all knowledge is only probable knowledge," or "knowledge is only warranted assertibility which is tested by how far it serves adaptation of an organism to its environment," or it may lead to the outright denial that there is any such thing as Reality or Truth. But in any case, certainty is lost with even the hope that certainty may ever be found. There are men of strange taste who seem to like the resultant gambler's world of complete uncertainty wherein nothing may be trusted and only illusions are left to feed the yearning for belief. But for all those of deeper religious need, the death of hope for certainty is the ultimate tragedy of absolute pessimism—not the rela-

tive pessimism of a Buddha, a Christ, or a Schopenhauer, who each saw the hopeless darkness of this dark
world as well as a Door leading to the undying Light,
but rather a pessimism so deep that there is no hope
for Light anywhere. Somewhere there must be certainty
if the end of life is to be more than eternal despair.
And to find this certainty something other than criticism is required.

As the stream of experience passes by us, we find no
beginning and no end. With our science we slash arbitrary cuts across that stream and find innumerable relations intertwining indeterminate parts that we can
define and organize into systems with considerable
skill. But as to the ultimate nature of the parts in relation we know nothing at all. From whence the stream
and whither? That is the question that centuries and
millenia of knowledge grounded only in the empirically
given has never been able to answer. Hopeless is the
estate of man if the source of all he knows is experience and nothing more.

But is there, mayhap, a source of knowledge other
than experience and its (supposedly) one-parented
child, the concept? The great among the ancients have
affirmed that there is, and so have others throughout
our racial history. I, too, affirm that there is this third
organ of knowledge and that it may be realized by him
who strives in the right direction. And I, also, confirm
those ancients who say that through this other organ
the resolution of the ultimate questions may be found
and a knowledge realized that is not sterile, though its
form may be most unexpected. But do the barricades
of modern criticism leave room for the forgotten Door?
I believe that they do, once the structure of criticism
is carefully analyzed and that which is sound is separated from that which is unsound. For philosophic

criticism is no authoritarian absolute competent to close the door to testimony from the fount of immediacy.

Kant's *Critique*[1] seems to have established this important proposition: The pure reason by itself can establish judgments of possibility only and can predicate existence of that possibility solely as a possibility. In order to predicate actuality of an existence, something more is required. In general, the predication of actual existence becomes possible by means of the empiric material given through the senses. The combination of the principles of pure reason and the material given through the senses makes possible the unity of experience whereby raw immediacy can be incorporated in a totality organized under law. This establishes a basis for confidence in the theoretic determinations of science as such, with all that follows from that. But there are demands within human consciousness that remain unsatisfied by this integration. Kant was aware of this fact and tried to resolve the problem in his *Critique of Practical Reason,* but he failed to achieve any adequate ground for assurance. Thus we stand today in a position where for thought there is no certain but only probable knowledge.

In the present philosophic outline I do not challenge the essential validity of the above conclusion, drawn from the *Critique of Pure Reason.* I accept the principle that *pure* thought can give only judgments of possible existence. But I go further than Kant in maintaining that in the total organization of consciousness there are phases that are neither conceptual nor empiric—the latter term being understood as consciousness-value dependent upon the senses. I draw attention to such a phase which, while not commonly active among men, has yet been reported by a few individuals throughout the span of known history, and maintain that I have myself realized at least some measure of the operation of this phase. This phase has been known in the West under a number of designations, such as "Cosmic Consciousness," "Mystical Insight," "Specialism," "Transhumanism," and so forth. In the Orient it has been given a more systematic treatment and designation. Thus, it is recognizable under the terms "Samadhi," "Dhyana," and "Prajna." The character of this phase of consciousness, as it has been represented in existent discussions and as revealed in my own contact with it, is of the nature of immediate awareness of an existential content or value. This immediacy is of a far superior order as compared to that given through the senses, for the latter is dependent upon the instrumentality of sensuous organs and functions. As compared to experience through the senses, this rarer phase of consciousness gives a transcendent value immediately and renders possible the predication of its existence in a judgment without violating the fundamental principles laid down by Kant.

An epistemological critique of this transcendental phase of consciousness is possible only by one in whom it is operative. This is true for the reason that the epistemologist, unlike the psychologist, can work only upon the material he actually has within his own consciousness. His is the inside view, while the psychologist, so long as he is only a psychologist, is restricted to the material that can be observed externally. Thus, the epistemologist is concerned with an analysis of the base of judgments of significance and value, while the method of the psychologist confines him to the field of judgments concerning empirically existent fact. As a consequence, the findings of the psychologist are irrelevant with respect to the more interior field of value and meaning. Failure to keep this fact in mind has produced a considerable confusion and heartache that were quite unnecessary.

The problem before us at this point is largely outside the reach of the psychologist, as it is concerned with value and meaning and not with observable existences, save only in very incidental degree. Very likely, the operation of the transcendental phase of consciousness which is predicated here, may have coordinate effects that can be observed by the psychologist, and perhaps even the physiologist. But whatever may be thus observed has no bearing upon the standing of the inner and directly realized value and meaning. Apparently, deviation from psychological and physiological norm may be, and indeed has been, noted. Often this deviation from norm has been interpreted as an adverse criticism of the directly realized meaningful content. This procedure is both unscientific and unphilosophical, for it involves the blind assumption that the virtue of being superior attaches to the norm as such. By applying this same method consistently within, say, the setting of the life and consciousness of the Australian bushmen, we would be forced to an adverse judgment relative to all the higher human culture in all forms. As many of our psychologists and physiologists do not actually maintain this consistent position, we are forced to the conclusion that they permit personal prejudice the determinant part in their valuations.

In current discussions it has been frequently noted that some concepts refer to sensuously given existences directly, while others do not. These existences have been called "referents." This leads to the formulation: Some concepts have referents while others do not. Generally the former concepts are given the superior validity and the latter only such validity as they may acquire by leading to concepts that do have referents. Indeed, there are some writers who deny that there is any such thing as a concept, and admit only words. In any case, the concepts, or words, without referents, are viewed as mere abstractions. Now, while it may be valid to regard concepts as important only in so far as they lead to referents, it is an arbitrary assumption to maintain that the referent must always be an empirically given fact. The referent may be a content given by the transcendent phase of consciousness immediately. In this case, the abstract concept may have as genuine reference-value as the more concrete ideas. It is only through the mystical awakening that this question can be answered positively. It is part of the thesis of the present work that abstract concepts, or at any rate some abstract concepts, do in fact mean a content that can be realized immediately. Thus the most abstract phase of thought can lead to meaning at least as directly as concrete ideas. But this meaning is not a sensuously given content.

A fundamental implication is that some conceptual systems may be regarded as *symbols* of transcendental meaning. Perhaps we may regard this symbolical form of reference as characteristic of all concepts with respect to all referents, whether empiric or transcendental. Some of the more mature branches of modern science seem to be arriving at such an interpretation of their own theoretical constructions. Thus, in current physics the constructions are often spoken of as models that mean a reality or referent that in its own nature is not thinkable. The model, then, is not a mere photographic reproduction but a thinkable and logical pattern that corresponds to the observed relationships in the referent. Such a pattern is a symbol, though perhaps not in the special sense in which Dr. C. G. Jung uses this term. At any rate, in this case it is a symbol of relationships. In the transcendental sense the symbol would represent substantialities. We have here, then, the essential difference between the intellect as used in science and as employed in connection with metaphysics. In the one case it supplies a symbol for relationships, in the other a symbol of substantial realities.

The primary value of the intellect is that it gives command. By means of science, nature is manipulated and controlled in an ever-widening degree. This fact is too well known to need elaboration. The same principle applies to transcendent realities. Through the power of thought this domain, too, becomes one that can be navigated. Immature mystics are not navigators, and therefore realize the transcendent as a sea in which their boats of consciousness either drift or are propelled by powers that they, individually, do not control. In such cases, if the boats are controlled, other unseen intelligence does the work. Many mystics give this controlling power the blanket name of "God." The real and genuine reference here is to a Power beyond the individual and self-conscious personal self that is realized as operative but not understood in its character. On the other hand, the mystic who has control may drop the term "God," with its usual connotations, from his vocabulary. However, he knows that the term does refer to something quite real though very imperfectly understood by the larger number of mystics. This control depends upon the development of understanding and thought having quite a different order of reference from that which applies to experience through the senses.

The empirically given manifold of fact that constitutes the raw material of physical science is not itself the same as science, nor does it become so simply by being collected, recorded, and classified. To raise this body of fact to the status of science it must *all* be incorporated within an interpretative theory that satisfies certain conditions. Two of these conditions are fundamental and ineluctable. First, the interpretative theory must be a logical and self-consistent whole from which deductive inferences can be drawn. This is an absolute necessity of science as such. Second, the theory must in addition be so selected and formulated that the sequential train of inferences therefrom shall at some stage suggest an empirically possible experiment or observation that can confirm or fail to confirm the inference. This condition is not a necessity of science in the ontological sense, but is an essential part of *empiric* science. This condition peculiarly marks the radical departure of modern science as contrasted to the science of the scholastics and of Aristotle. It is a principle of the highest pragmatic importance and is the prime key to the western and modern type of control of nature. Now, any organization of a collection of observed facts that satisfies these two conditions is science in the current sense of the word.

But while the above two principles are the only two necessary conditions for defining a body of knowledge as scientific, in the current sense, yet in practice scientists demand more. There is a third condition that serves convenience and even prejudice rather than logic. This is the requirement that the interpretative theory shall be congruent with already established or accepted scientific points of view, unless it is well proven that this third condition cannot be satisfied without violating the first or second. The long resistance to the acceptance of the Einstein dynamics was due to the fact that the relativity theory violated the third condition, though conforming to the first two.

Only with reluctance could the body of scientists be induced to abandon the classical mechanics of Newton. For many years the latter was lovingly patched with the baling wire of *ad hoc* hypotheses, and the body of scientists—very much like a conservative farmer attached to a tumbledown wagon, ancient team, and disintegrating harness, held together and kept going by every device of ingenuity, and hating the modern truck that has been offered him as a present—refused to have anything to do with the new theory, even though it satisfied the first condition with exceptional beauty. But ultimately, because the relativity theory met the test of the second condition and the Newtonian view had indubitably lost its logical coherence in the domain of electrodynamics, due to heavy patching, the former was, perforce, accepted. This bit out of the history of science simply illustrates the fact that the third condition is merely arbitrary in the logical sense. However, it must be acknowledged that this condition does have a degree of practical and psychological justification. It is part and parcel of the conservative spirit that someone has given a rather aphoristic formulation in the following terms: "So long as it is not *necessary* to change, it is necessary *not* to change." Change that is too rapid for adjustment and assimilation is not without its danger.

The danger of change is a danger to the all-too-human nature of the scientist and not a danger to science itself. The third condition exists for the protection of the scientist because he is a human being, and is quite irrelevant so far as science as such is concerned. I have talked to scientifically oriented minds and developed conceptions implying or explicitly affirming the reality of the transcendent, to which they took no logical exception, but they then drew the protecting robes of the third condition about themselves and withdrew to what they imagined was the safety of their enclosure. It is not wise to treat scared children too roughly, and in so far as the third condition is used as a protective temenos for the fallible human nature of the scientist, it should be respected. But this third condition is no real part of science as science and may not be properly invoked to discredit the *truth* of any interpretative construction.

Today in the vast domain of the biopsychological sciences—which include the whole of man in so far as he is an object for science—and in much of philosophy, the predominant orientation is to Darwin. Darwinism has a twofold meaning, the lesser aspect of which is innocent and creditable enough, but the larger aspect of which is a sinister force—perhaps the most sinister—that seriously threatens the ultimate good of the human soul.

In the narrower sense, Darwin gave us a major scientific contribution. Through the facts observed by Darwin the notion of organic evolution is drawn into the focus of consciousness with a well-nigh ineluctable force. So far the contribution of Darwin is positive and, I believe, permanent. But in the larger sense Darwinism involves a good deal more than this. The evolutionary process is interpreted as a blind and mechanical force operating in the primordial roots of life and responsible for every development, including man, even the most cultured. The facts may, and I believe do, require some conception of evolution for their interpretation. But there are other conceptions of the nature of evolution, differing radically from Darwin's idea, that do interpret the facts, or may be adapted to such interpretation. Evolution may be conceived as the technique of an intelligent process, and it may be conceived comprehensively as the complement of an involutionary process. Evolution thus conceived is not part of Darwinism in the invidious sense.

The first two conditions of scientific method do not impose the blind and mechanical view of evolution as a scientifically necessary interpretation. The orientation on the part of scientists to this radically antitranscendental view is merely in conformity with the artificial third condition. Yet it must be confessed that the mechanistic interpretation does have certain advantages. To those who hate mystery it seems as though here we have a key for understanding life, in all its elaborations, that is directly and objectively understandable. Thus the senses and the intellect are all that is necessary for the conquest of life. There is much of illusion in this. For when the biologist falls back on the chemist to explain his vital phenomena, the chemist gives him cold comfort when he says that he does not find chemical phenomena adequate to meet the requirements of the biologist; and then when the biologist turns to the most basic physical science of all, i.e., physics, he finds that since 1896 physics has laid the foundation for mysticism with a vengeance, and the materialistic biologist is left without fundamental support for his interpretative view.

The idea that in the purely naturalistic sense there is a tendency in living organism to rise in the scale is by no means a scientifically established fact. To be sure, we do find a vast difference of level in the hierarchy of living creatures, reaching from the mineral or near the mineral to the Buddhas, but it is not a scientifically established fact that this difference of elevation is not due to periodic or continuous impingement of energy from transcendental roots. If the cause of rise in the scale is transcendental, then it is not *naturalistic*.[2] Apart from this consideration—which for the moment

I shall treat as only speculative—there is strong positive evidence that in the purely naturalistic sense all function in nature tends toward degradation. The physicists tell us that in all their observation from the laboratory up to astrophysics they find no exception to the second law of thermodynamics. In simple terms, this law says that all energy tends to flow down hill, that is, from centers of high concentration to regions of low concentration, as from the stars to the depths of space. And further, energy is available for work only while it is on this flow, and is lost in the final stage of dissemination. All this simply leads to the view that the purely naturalistic tendency is toward degradation.

Are we not justified in viewing life as some kind of energy? Would not such a view be a peculiarly consistent application of the third condition? Because it constitutes an extension of an already accepted scientific viewpoint. But if natural life is to be viewed as an energy, is there not then a strong presumption that this energy does *not* constitute an exception to the general law, which seems to be universally confirmed by the observation of the physicist? If the answer to these three questions is affirmative, it follows that we must view natural life, taken in isolation from any transcendental impingement of energy, as tending toward degradation. The consequences of such an altered viewpoint are far reaching. For instance, the ethnologist would no longer find justification for viewing the culture of so-called primitive man as the interpretatively significant root-source of higher culture, since this primitive culture would actually be degraded culture and thus not a root but the near end-term of a process of degradation. We would no longer be justified in viewing something like the voodoo as the primitive form of religious consciousness, or the seed from which ultimately flowered the higher religious consciousness, but we would see in this form of religious practice the degraded state of religion—that which religion becomes in the hands of a race moving toward extinction. As another instance we would find that the reductive interpretation in analytic psychology would lose all really significant value.[3]

Later in this volume I shall have occasion to develop more fully the line of argument sketched above in its relation to much current psychological interpretation of mystical states of consciousness. For it appears that most of the disparagement found in such interpretations develops from the prejudicial attitude growing out of a predeliction for the invidious extension of Darwinism. For the present I am concerned only with the development of a general orienting preview in relation to the general reference of ideas.

The following chapter is introduced to establish a ground of knowledge upon which the body of subsequent interpretation is largely based. This mainly descriptive-narrative statement is to be understood as having the same methodological significance that attaches to the laboratory record in the development of scientific theoretical interpretation. But in this case the immediately given material is not of the objective sort studied in scientific laboratories; it is that which is found by a predominantly conscious penetration of the subjective pole of consciousness. In this case that which corresponds to the raw material of scientific theory is the qualities or states found by piercing into the 'I' rather than by observing the 'not-I'. A referential ground for interpretation of this sort is far from being a commonplace in the sense that all the objective material of scientific theory may be called commonplace, since the latter is, in principle, available to any so-called five-sense consciousness. Very few human beings have conscious familiarity with the zone in question, but there are a few who do, and they understand each other when they meet. This latter fact is of the very highest significance, for it reveals that the subjective realm is not something absolutely unique in an individual and having nothing in common with anyone else. Unquestionably there are detailed features of the subjective zone that are unique, as one individual is contrasted with another individual and as one type of individual is set off by another type. But these variants grow less and less with the depth of penetration, while there is a progressive growth in congruency of insight that in the end tends to become absolute. At the very center stands Enlightenment, which is fundamentally the same for all men. I must leave this statement in dogmatic form since it can neither be proved nor disproved in objective terms.

The initial and most superficial stage of the subjective penetration is, admittedly, intensely personal, for no man can start at any point save that of himself, a concrete individual living at some particular point in time and space. An early danger of the Way is that of becoming entrapped in this purely personal subjectivity for an indefinite period of time. But he who is caught at this point has scarcely taken the first step on the ladder. The real penetration lies beyond the personal self. Reaching beyond the personal stage the 'I' rapidly grows in impersonality until it acquires the value of a Universal Principle. Thus the inner ground is a common ground just as truly as is the objective content of consciousness common to all men. As empiric scientists, in general, understand each other's way of thinking, so those who know some measure of the impersonal 'I' understand each other's peculiar language, at least in its primary reference. To be sure, there are variants here, just as there are differences of scientific specialty, that restrict the completeness of mutual understanding. In general, a specialist in subatomic physics would not talk the specific language of a specialist in biology, yet with respect to the general determinants of empirical science as such there is mutuality of understanding. The analogue of this is definitely to be found among the mystics. And this fact is a real cause for confusion on the part of a non-mystical investigator of mystical states of consciousness. There are agreements and differentiations not hard for him who has Vision to understand, but that are hopelessly confusing to the uninitiated.

In the record given in the next chapter, part of the material is doubtless unique with respect to the individual. In this respect there are several divergences from other records that can be found in literature. But very soon the content acquires a progressively universal character. Proof of this can be found, likewise, by reference to the appropriate literature. It is this more universally identical content that constitutes the main ground of reference of the later interpretation. Indeed, there is here a common ground for all men, but generally it is lost in the Unconscious, yet waiting, ever ready to be revealed when the Light of Consciousness turns upon Itself toward Its Source.

Notes to Chapter 1

1. *The Critique of Pure Reason* by Immanuel Kant, the most important work in the whole of western philosophical literature.

2. "Naturalism" here is taken to mean the theory that sensuously observed Nature is *all* that there is of Reality.

3. In analytic psychology the standpoint that views the reference of complexes welling up from the unconscious as being due to causal factors that lie in the conscious field of the past is called "reductive." This stands in contrast to the "constructive" standpoint that views such complexes as symbolically meaning, or also meaning, an end to be developed in the future. See "Definitions," Chapter XI, in Jung's *Psychological Types.*

Chapter 2

A
MYSTICAL
UNFOLDMENT

●

It was during the period when I was a student in the
Graduate School of Philosophy of Harvard University
in 1912–13 that, finally, I became convinced of the
probable existence of a transcendent mode of consciousness that could not be comprehended within the
limits of our ordinary forms of knowledge. Several factors converged in the forming of this conviction. For
one thing, a considerable portion of western philosophy from the Greeks to the present day seemed to
imply some sort of insight into Reality that was not
reducible to observation or derivable from immediate

experience by logical deduction, however acute the course of reasoning might be. At the same time, the profound assurance of truth I had realized in my studies in pure mathematics did not seem to be explained satisfactorily by any of those philosophical interpretations that aim to show that mathematics is derived from the facts of the external world by mere abstraction. Throughout all discussion the feeling persisted that at the root of mathematics there lay a mystery, reaching far deeper than anything attained through the senses. In addition, for a period of some three years I had had a degree of contact with the Buddhist, Vedantist, and Theosophical phases of oriental thought, and in all these the evidence of some sort of transcendental consciousness was peculiarly decisive. On the other hand, as a factor that acted in a sort of negative sense, the various philosophies that repudiated the actuality of any transcendental or mystical reality seemed to have the effect of barrenness, which left them far from satisfactory. Meanwhile, acting beneath the surface of my consciousness, there was a more or less inarticulate faith that insisted that the truly valid interpretation of reality must be such as would satisfy through and through, and thus not be barren. Yet the dialectical and polemical processes of the various western schools of thought were inadequate for supplying the completely satisfactory solution that, while affording the appropriate recognition of the needs of experience and of reason, at the same time satisfied the hunger for assurance and depth. However, the evidence from history seemed to make it clear that at least some few among mankind had achieved this assurance, which was both reasonable and full. So it seemed to me to be highly probable that there must be a mode of consciousness or knowledge not yet comprehended by epistemology and psychology as developed in the West.

At that time I had no clear idea of what this knowledge might be, or of the methods by which one might hope to attain it. I had had some brief contact with the oriental manuals on transformation and realized that they seemed to point to a kind of consciousness that, while not generally realized by mankind, yet was potentially within the range of human attainment. At first I attempted to interpret the material contained within these manuals in the conceptual forms of western thought, but always in these efforts I finally met failure. I soon found enough to know that there was something concealed within the manuals, because I noted certain subtle affective changes they induced within me, and there was aroused also a sense of something near that yet defeated the efforts of my understanding to comprehend. So I began to feel sure of a hidden somewhat to which these manuals were related, if for no other reason than that their first effect was to leave me disturbed and restless. The desire for peace of mind sometimes counseled me to turn away from them, but then the realization that the subsequent position would be arbitrary and artificial, and therefore a repudiation of an honest search for reality, whatever that might be, always forced me to return to those disturbing manuals.

It soon became clear, if this search in a new direction was to be successful, I had to reach beyond anything contained within the academic circles of the West. The manuals demanded a life-practice or attitude that involved the whole man, and thus the requirements were incompatible with the attitude of a tentative *trying*, while part of the man stood back enclosed in a sort of reserve. Again and again I found the statement that, if a man would attain the transcendent realization, he must renounce all, and not merely part, of what he personally is. I did not find this an easy step to consummate. For years I resisted it, offering part of myself, yet holding back a certain reserve. During all this time I realized only imperfect and unsatisfactory results, and often regretted the experiment. But it was not long before I found that I had gone too far to turn back. I had realized enough to render forever barren the old pastures, and yet not enough to know either peace or satisfaction. For some years I rested in this position of indecision, without achieving much visible progress. Yet meanwhile, as time rolled on, progressive exhaustion of the world-desire developed, while concomitantly there grew a greater willingness to abandon all that had been reserved and so complete the experiment.

As the years passed, I began to form a better idea of the goal and of the reasons underlying the requirements of the manuals. All this helped to arouse a greater will to effort, and so I began to experiment more deliberately with the various transformation techniques that came before my attention. All, or nearly all, these were of oriental origin, and in most cases I found them disappointing in their effectiveness. But, finally, I realized that there are several techniques and that these are designed to meet the needs of quite various temperaments and psychical organizations. In time, it became clear that there are important temperamental and psychical differences as between orientals and occidentals, and that this fact implied modification of methods. So I began seeking for the invariable elements in the different techniques, with a view to finding just what was essential. Ultimately, I found one oriental Sage with whose thought and temperament I felt a high degree of sympathetic rapport. This Sage was the Vedantic philosopher known as Shankara. I found myself in striking agreement with the more fundamental phases of his thought and quite willing to apply the highly intellectual technique that he had charted. It was in this Sage's writings that I finally found the means that were effective in producing the transformation I sought.

In the meantime I had met various individuals and groups who offered and rendered assistance in the direction I was seeking to go, and from all of them I must acknowledge having received positive values which had a progressively clarifying effect upon the understanding. But none of them offered methods that proved decisively effective with me. Nearly all these placed their predominant stress upon feeling-transformation and failed to satisfy the intellectual demands that, with me, always remained strong. Of all such Teachers whom I met, either through their living presence or their written word, Shankara, alone, adequately satisfied the intellectual side of my nature. So, while I owe much to many whom I have known in one way or another, it yet remained for Shankara to offer the hint that proved to be decisive.

However, even Shankara did not supply all the specifications for the method that became finally effective. Also, I had to discover adaptations that would satisfy the needs of an academically trained occidental nature. None of these adaptations violated any of the fundamentals of Shankara's teaching. But what I added as a sort of creative discovery was peculiarly decisive in its effect. At the present time, I am convinced that some such original discovery is vitally important in effecting a self-induced transformation.

In the period just preceding the hour when success finally crowned a search that covered nearly a quarter of a century, certain features characteristic of the transcendent consciousness had become theoretically clear. I had attained an intellectual grasp of the vitally important fact that transcendent consciousness differs from our ordinary consciousness in the primary respect that it is a state of consciousness wherein the disjunction between the subject to consciousness and the object of consciousness is destroyed. It is a state wherein self-identity and the field of consciousness are blended in one indissoluble whole. This supplied the prime characteristic by which all our common consciousness could be differentiated from the transcendent. The former is all of the type that may be called subject-object or relative consciousness.

The second fact of primary importance, that I now understand, was that the common denominator, as it were, of both kinds of consciousness lay in the subject or self. This fact is identical, in a significant degree, with the fundamental discovery of Descartes, i.e., that when everything is submitted to critical examination it still remains impossible to doubt one's own being, however little one may be able to understand the nature of that being. I also discovered the essential timelessness of the subject, or self, and that in its purity, unmixed with any objective element, it can never truly be an *object* of consciousness. I readily realized that if pure subjectivity, or the bare power to be aware, was a permanent or unchanging element and therefore must, as a consequence, stand outside of time and be unaffected by any history, then it must be, of necessity, immortal. I saw that this kind of immortality is wholly impersonal and does not, by itself, imply the unlimited persistence of the quality of individuality that distinguishes one man from another. But the finding of one immortal element affords a definite anchorage and security, grounded in certainty of an order far superior to that of any kind of faith. When I had reached this point in the unfoldment of my understanding, I really had achieved the positive value of decisive importance that, some years later, was to prove the effective entering wedge for opening the Way to the transcendent level of consciousness.

While, in addition to the principles or facts just discussed, there are a number of other statements relative to the transcendent that can be found in literature, yet, in my judgment, the recognition of these is all that is absolutely essential to prepare the understanding for the Transcendental Awakening. These principles or facts are clearly of noetic value, and they can be appreciated quite apart from any affective transformation that may be associated with the arousing of transcendental apperception. In fact, it may be entirely possible that a sufficiently concentrated meditation upon the inner significance of these principles might prove an efficient means for effecting the transformation without the aid of any other subsidiary factor. However, they were not the sole factors that were operative in my experience, though they occupied the position of first importance.

Concurrently with the attainment of the preliminary noetic adjustment, certain important transformations were developing in the affective and conative side of my nature. Early in my studies I found that the manuals emphasized the necessity of killing out desire. This proved to be a difficult step to understand and far from easy to accomplish. Desire and sentient life are inseparable, and so it seemed as though this demand implied the equivalent of self-extinction. It was only after some time that I discovered that the real meaning consisted in a changing of the polarization of desire. Ordinarily, desire moves toward objects and objective achievements, in some sense. It is necessary that this desire should be given another polarization so that, instead of objects and achievements in the world-field being sought, an eternal and all-encompassing consciousness should be desired. This interpretation clarified the meaning of the demand and rendered it intellectually acceptable, but did not at once effect the required repolarization. To accomplish this the wearing power of time proved to be necessary. As the years passed, the outward polarization of the desire did grow weaker, and some months just prior to the hour when the radical transition in consciousness was consummated, it actually had become transformed into a distaste for practically everything belonging to the world-field. It seemed that all in the world-field was drained dry of every significant value. Though there still remained vast quantities of objective secular information of which I was ignorant and that I could have acquired, and there were many experiences that I had never sampled, yet I realized that, as such, they were void of depth and had no more value than David Hume's game of backgammon. If there had not been a compensating polarization of desire in another direction, it seems highly probable that at this stage my state of consciousness would have had a very pessimistic and depressed coloring, but as there was at the same time a strong growth of the desire for transcendent consciousness, the result was that the psychical energy did have an outlet. However, there was a critical point at which the shifting polarization had attained something like a neutral balance.[1] At this point there was no decisive wish to go either way and the whole field of interest took on a colorless quality. As I look back upon the whole experience, I would say that this stage was the only one that involved real danger. I found it necessary to supplement the neutral state of desire by a forcibly willed resolution, and thus proceed in the chosen direction regardless of the absence of inclination.[2] However, once past the critical point, the inward polarization of desire developed rapidly, and presently spontaneous inclination rendered the forcibly willed resolution unnecessary.

In addition to the barrier of desire directed toward external objects, the manuals specify a very important and closely related barrier to attainment. This is egoism. The strong feeling for, and attachment to, egoistic differentiation is an insurmountable barrier to a kind of consciousness that, instead of being discrete and ego bound, is continuous, free, and impersonal. So a certain critical degree of dissolution or solution of the egoistic crystallization must be effected if the transformation of consciousness is to be successful. I did not find it difficult to appreciate the logic of this requirement, but again, as in the case of outwardly polarized desire, the difficult part was the actual dissolution of the egoistic feeling. The ordinary technique is the practice of practical altruism until personal self-consideration sinks well into the background. But this is not the only means that effects this result. A desire for the transcendent Self and a love of universals also tend toward the required melting of the egoistic feeling. In this part of the discipline I found that my already established love of mathematics and philosophy was an aid of radical importance that, supplemented by more tangible practices, finally produced the requisite degree of melting.

In my experience, the preliminary noetic adjustment required much less time and effort than the requisite affective and conative reorientation. With the latter, the wearing-down process of time proved to be necessary. Unquestionably, if the feelings and will could have been made to respond more readily to the leadership of understanding, then the transformation of the consciousness would have been achieved in much less time. But, as human nature is constituted, it appears this phase of the labor does require much patience and the assistance of the maturing that time brings in its natural course.

Preceding the hour of the radical transition in consciousness, there had been two premonitory recognitions of substantial adjustment value. The first occurred about fourteen years before, and the second only about nine months prior to, the culminating stage. The first of these illustrates the important difference between the theoretical appreciation of a fact or principle and a kind of adjustment to, or realization of, that which I have called "Recognition." For some years I had been familiar with the Indian concept of Atman and understood that it meant a spiritual 'Self' conceived as being the irreducible center of consciousness on which all knowledge or consciousness in the relative sense depended. I had found no empiric or logical difficulty with this concept and had accepted it as valid. I understood quite well, as an immediate implication, that since I am the Self, therefore, the judgment "I am Atman" is practically a tautology. I did not see how any idea could have greater philosophical clarity. But on one occasion, when a friend was outlining a method of systematic discrimination between the Self and the not-Self, finally culminating in the judgment "I am Atman," I recognized in this a profound truth carrying the very highest significance. With this there came a sense of new insight and of joy. It made a difference in me that the theoretical acceptance and appreciation of the judgment had failed to do.

In analyzing the difference between the recognition and the theoretical acceptance without recognition, it seems that in the latter instance there is a quality that might be called mediative distance, while in the case of recognition there is the closeness of immediacy. There is something nonlogical that is added, but, while nonlogical, it is not antilogical. Part of the effect was an increased clarity in the apperception of the logical implications that followed. Spontaneously and with intellectual ease I began thinking consequences that were practically identical with a number of fundamental statements in the *Bhagavad-Gita*. But now these thoughts were my thoughts in a close and intimate sense, whereas prior to that time they were simply ideas that I had touched through my reading, often not feeling very sympathetic with them. Within a considerable range of consciousness I now felt assurance, whereas previously I had merely believed or accepted because of theoretical considerations. Ideas that formerly had had the effect of constraint upon me now had a definitely joyous and freedom-giving value. And it was only a momentary flash of insight that had made all this difference! The effect persisted and has never been lost at any time since, though the freshness of the insight gradually waned and became a "matter of course" in the background of my thinking and valuation. Much that had been previously obscure in a certain class of oriental thinking I now found myself understanding with a greatly increased clarity.[3]

In connection with the foregoing recognition, it seems clear to me that the prior theoretical acceptance has prepared the soil of the mind, as it were, for the subsequent realization. While there is something additional in the recognition as compared to the theoretical acceptance, that "something" is not in the nature of concepts nor of an added experience in any perceptive sense. It rather belongs to some other dimension of consciousness, not contained in either concepts or percepts, but which has a radical effect upon value. It may lead a train of thought to new discovery, but is not itself revealed in a subsequent analysis of that train of thought. The formal relationships of the final expression of the thought may be quite clear and understandable to the trained intellect of a man who is without insight and they may stand up quite well under criticism. Yet the insight renders possible much that is beyond the power of the trained intellect that lacks the insight. It can lead the way in radical cognitive discovery and contribute a form to the time-bound world that will have its effects, large or small, in the stream of time. But he who is blind to this dimension of consciousness that I have called "Value" will see only a form, a mere configuration on the surface. Yet another who is awake to Value will, at the same time, recognize depth in the configuration. Also, one who is not awakened may, by dwelling upon the configuration through a method that has long been known as meditation, find the value-dimension aroused to recognition in his consciousness. And it is just this something additional, this somewhat that is over and above the concept, with all its traceable ramifications, that makes all the difference in the world!

The second premonitory recognition had a markedly different background, since it expressed itself in a judgment for which I had not been prepared by prior theoretical acceptance. I had been meditating upon the concept of "Nirvana" when, suddenly, it dawned upon me that I, in the inmost sense, am identical with Nirvana. My previous ideas upon this subject had involved a confusion that, while logical analysis should have dispelled it, none the less persisted. Despite statements to the contrary, with which I was familiar, I had been thinking of Nirvana as a kind of other world standing in disparate relation to this world of relative consciousness. Of course, I should have realized the hidden error in this view, as such an interpretation involved placing Nirvana in the relative manifold. But probably through intellectual laziness I failed to carry my thought through on this point. The result was that the recognition effected for me a new cognitive discovery as well as a deepening and illumining effect in the dimension of value. I readily saw the reason why so little had been said, and indeed why so little could be said, concerning Nirvana beyond the assertion of its reality. The inner core of the 'I', like Nirvana, is not an objective existence but is, rather, the 'thread' upon which the objective material of consciousness is strung. Relative consciousness deals with the objective material but never finds the 'thread' as an object. Yet it is that 'thread' that renders all else possible. In fact, it is the most immediate and ever-present reality of all. Nirvana, like the 'I', cannot be located anywhere, as in a distinct place, for it is at once everywhere and nowhere, both in space and time. Upon this 'thread', space and time are strung just as truly as all perceptual experience and all thought consciousness and any other mode of relative consciousness there may be.

This second recognition had implications that actually were to become clear to me at the deepest stage of realization some ten months later. Presumptively, a sufficiently acute thought would have developed the consequences beforehand, but I failed to do this. At any rate, I now see that this second recognition contained the seed of insight that renders clear the Buddhist doctrine of anatman, which in turn constitutes an important part of the central core of that philosophy, as well as one of its most obscure doctrines.[4] But I shall return to this point at a later time when the ground for its discussion has been better prepared.

For the last two or three years prior to the culminating transition in consciousness, I was aware of a decrease in my intellectual capacity. The meaning of philosophic and mathematical literature that formerly had been within the range of my working consciousness became obscure. The effort to understand much that I had formerly understood reasonably well simply produced drowsiness. At the time this caused me considerable concern, and I wondered whether it might be a sign of premature intellectual aging. However, it proved to be a passing phase, for shortly prior to the culminating point the intellectual alertness returned, and after that point it became more acute than it ever had been. The recognition, among other effects, proved to have the value of an intellectual rejuvenation. I mention this development since it seems to have some significance. When observed retrospectively it would seem that there had been a withdrawal of the personal energy from the intellectual field into some level that was not consciously traceable. As yet, I have not found any records of an analogous experience on the part of others when approaching the mystical crisis. I am noting this development for such value as it may ultimately prove to have.[5]

During the last few weeks just preceding the transformation, there grew within me a strong expectation and a kind of inner excitement. I felt within me an indefinable assurance that, at last, the culminating success of a long search was within reach. I felt that I was near the discovery of the means whereby I could surmount the apparently unscalable walls that seemed to lie all about. I had been studying and meditating upon the philosophic writings of Shankara more seriously than at any prior time and sensed that in them was to be found the vital key. At the same time I had a strong desire for a period of solitude. Presently the opportunity came to satisfy this desire, and taking a volume of Shankara's translated works with me, I spent several days in a wild and lonely place.[6] The study and thought of this period proved to be decisively effective. As a result of this effort an idea of cardinal importance was evolved in my mind. In this case, as in that of the first premonitory recognition, the value of the idea did not inhere in its being something new to thought as such. It exists in literature, and I had come across it in my reading, but at the time in question it came with the force of a new discovery in a matrix of assurance and with an affective quality that I can hardly express in any other way than to say it was "Light." While the moment of this discovery was not that of the culminating recognition, yet I have reason to believe that it was the critical or turning point that rendered the final recognition accessible. It altered the base of thought and valuation in a profound way and in a direction confirmed by the subsequent realization. Because of the important part this idea played, a brief elucidation of it seems necessary.

It is a common, and apparently quite natural, habit with us to regard the material given through the senses as being something actual. Our science and philosophy may fail to give an adequate interpretation of this material, but still we generally feel sure that it is something. So the larger portion of the human search for Reality is in the field of the things given to our consciousness through the senses. But in my reflecting upon the idea that this universe of things is derived from and dependent upon a primordial plenum, it suddenly struck me that in the midst of the bare and original fullness there could be nothing to arouse discrete or concrete consciousness. It is a familiar fact of psychology that a long-continued or unchanging state or quality tends to become unconscious. Thus, in a state of health an individual is only slightly conscious of his body in its organic functioning. But let there be some form of injury or sickness, and at once the individual is conscious of his organism as he was not before. Likewise, when a long-continued period of bodily pain has ceased, there is then a concrete consciousness of well-being such as did not exist before the pain. In such a case, simply to be free of the pain has the value of an active joy, though the same bodily state did not have that value formerly. Through pain the joy-consciousness of health was aroused to recognition. Now, applying this principle in an ontological sense, it follows that the Consciousness of the original Fullness can only be aroused by first passing through the experience of 'absence' or 'emptiness', in some degree. Thus the active, concrete, and perceptual consciousness is to be viewed as an arousal of specific awareness through a partial blanking out of the full and perfectly balanced consciousness of the Primordial State. As a result, the world of things, apparently given through the senses, is actually a domain of relative emptiness. We become concretely aware only when contacting voids. There is nothing in this to invalidate the positive findings of natural science. Science studies the direct or indirect determinations of the senses and finds those relationships binding the various parts that render possible the formulation of laws. The question as to whether the terms or facts of science have a substantial base, and if so, what its nature is, is a metaphysical question quite beyond the range of the methodology of natural science. Scientific philosophy reveals a real critical acumen in dropping the notion of "substance" as being relevant to our kind of science. It says—I think correctly—that science is concerned with terms in various relations, and nothing else. When it goes further than that and says specifically or in effect that scientific knowledge is the only kind of real knowledge possible to man, or possible at all, it trips on the very error it charges against certain other philosophies, i.e., that of "definition by initial predication."

Now, if it is relative emptiness that arouses to activity concrete consciousness, then it follows that actual substantiality is inversely proportional to sensibility or ponderability. There is most substance where the senses find least, and vice versa. Thus the terms-in-relation of the sensible world are to be viewed as relative emptiness contained in an unseen and substantial matrix. From this there follows, at once, a very important consequence. The discrete manifoldness and apparent pluralism of sensibly given things are quite compatible with a continuous and unitary substantial matrix. The monistic tendency of interpretations based upon mystical insight at once becomes clear, and here is afforded a reconciliation of the one and the many.[7]

It is not my purpose, at the present time, to enter upon an adequate philosophical defense of this interpretation, but simply to present the idea that was of decisive psychological importance with me in removing a barrier to mystical realization. At least, the validity of this idea was, and still remains, clear to me as an individual.

The idea I had just recognized made possible an effective conceptual reorientation. The totality of being had become divided into two phases. The higher phase I called the 'substantial' or 'transcendental.' This was supersensible and monistic, and served as the base in which the lower phase inhered. The latter phase thus became, by contrast, the sensible and phenomenal world, existing only through a complete dependence upon the supersensible and substantial. Within the latter existed endless multiplicity and divisibility.

There remained now merely the clearing up of the residual barriers to the complete identification of the self with the supersensible and substantial world, accompanied by the thorough divorcement of the self-identity with the phenomenal world. But a few days were required for the completion of this effort. Meanwhile, I had returned from physical solitude to the active concerns of social life, although I remained in a state of considerable mental detachment and continued brooding. Finally, on the seventh of August, 1936, after having completed the reading of Shankara's discussion of "Liberation," as given in the *System of the Vedanta* by Paul Deussen, I entered upon a course of meditative reflection upon the material just read.[8] While engaged in this course of reflection, it suddenly dawned upon me that a common error in meditation—and one which I had been making right along—lay in the seeking of a subtle object or experience. Now, an object or an experience, no matter how subtle, remains a phenomenal time-space existence and therefore is other than the supersensible substantiality. Thus the consciousness to be sought is the state of pure subjectivity without an object. This consideration rendered clear to me the emphasis, repeatedly stated by the manuals, upon the closing out of the modifications of the mind. But I had never found it possible completely to silence thought. So it occurred to me that success might be attained simply by a discriminative isolation of the subjective pole of consciousness, with the focus of consciousness placed upon this aspect, but otherwise leaving the mental processes free to continue in their spontaneous functioning—they, however, remaining in the periphery of the attentive consciousness. Further, I realized that pure subjective consciousness without an object must appear to the relative consciousness to have objects. Hence Recognition did not, of itself, imply a new experiential content in consciousness.[9] I saw that genuine Recognition is simply a realization of Nothing, but a Nothing that is absolutely substantial and identical with the SELF. This was the final turn of the Key that opened the Door. I found myself at once identical with the Void-ness, Darkness, and Silence, but realized them as utter, though ineffable, Fullness, in the sense of Substan-tiality, Light, in the sense of Illumination, and Sound, in the sense of pure formless Meaning and Value. The deepening of consciousness that followed at once is sim-ply inconceivable and quite beyond the possibility of adequate representation. To suggest the Value of this transcendental state of consciousness requires concepts of the most intensive possible connotation and the modes of expression that indicate the most superlative value art can devise.[10] Yet the result of the best effort seems a sorry sort of thing when compared with the immediate Actuality. All language, as such, is defeated when used as an instrument of portrayal of the trans-cendent.

There are implications and consequences following from such an insight that do fall within the range of formulation, and in this a man who has the appro-priate skill can certainly do more than one who has little knowledge of the art of expression. But the imme-diate noetic and affective values of the insight, while they may be directly realized, cannot be conveyed by any formulation or representation whatsoever.

A *definite line of demarcation must be drawn be-tween the transcendental state of consciousness itself and the precipitated effects within the relative con-sciousness.* The former is not an experience, but a Recognition or an Awakening on a timeless level of consciousness. The latter is an effect precipitated into the time-world and therefore has experiential and rela-tive value. At the final moment, I was prepared not to have the personal, time-bound man share in any of the values that might inhere in the insight. But, very quickly, values began to descend into the outer consciousness and have continued to do so, more or less periodically, to the present day. These precipitated values have much that is of definite noetic content and decided affective value, well within the range of expression.

The listing and delineation of the elements that were precipitated into the relative consciousness from the first stage of insight is the next step.[11]

1. The first discernible effect in consciousness was something that I may call a *shift in the base of consciousness*. From the relative point of view, the final step may be likened to a leap into Nothing. At once, that Nothing was resolved into utter Fullness, which in turn gave the relative world a dreamlike quality of unreality. I felt and knew myself to have arrived, at last, at the Real. I was not dissipated in a sort of spatial emptiness, but on the contrary was spread out in a Fullness beyond measure. The roots of my consciousness, which prior to this moment had been (seemingly) more or less deeply implanted in the field of relative consciousness, now were forcibly removed and instantaneously transplanted into a supernal region. This sense of being thus transplanted has continued to the present day, and it seems to be a much more normal state of emplacement than ever the old rooting had been.

2. Closely related to the foregoing is a *transformation in the meaning of the 'Self,' or 'I'*. Previously, pure subjectivity had seemed to me to be like a zero or vanishing point, a somewhat that had position in consciousness but no body. So long as that which man calls his 'self' had body, it stood within the range of analytic observation. Stripping off the sheaths of this body until none is left is the function of the discriminative technique in meditation. At the end there remains

that which is never an object and yet is the foundation upon which all relative consciousness is strung like beads upon a string. As a symbol to represent this ultimate and irreducible subject to all consciousness, the 'I' element, I know nothing better than zero or an evanescent point. The critical stage in the transformation is the realization of the 'I' as zero. But, at once, that 'I' spreads out into an unlimited "thickness." It is as though the 'I' became the whole of space. The Self is no longer a pole or focal point, but it sweeps outward, everywhere, in a sort of unpolarized consciousness, which is at once self-identity and the objective content of consciousness. It is an unequivocal transcendence of the subject-object relationship. Herein lies the rationale of the inevitable ineffability of mystical insight. All language is grounded in the subject-object relationship, and so, at best, can only misrepresent transcendent consciousness when an effort is made to express its immediately given value.

3. There is a sense of enormous *depth penetration* with two phases barely distinguishable during this first stage of insight. The first phase is highly noetic but superconceptual.[12] I had awareness of a kind of thought of such an enormous degree of abstraction and universality that is was barely discernible as being of noetic character. If we were to regard our most abstract concepts as being of the nature of tangible bodies, containing a hidden but substantial meaning, then this transcendent thought would be of the nature of the meaning without the conceptual embodiment. It is the compacted essence of thought, the "sentences" of which would require entire lifetimes for their elaboration in objective form and yet remain unexhausted at the conclusion of such effort. In my relative consciousness I knew that I was thinking such massive thoughts, and I felt the infiltration of value from them. In a

curious way I knew that *I* KNEW in cosmical proportions. However, no brain substance could be so refined as to be capable of attunement to the grand cosmical tread of those Thoughts.

But still beyond the thoughts of cosmic proportions and illimitable abstraction there were further deeps transcending the furthest reaches of noetic and affective value. Yet, in this, the self-identity remained unbroken in a dimly sensed series of deeps reaching on to ever greater profundities of what, in one sense, was an impenetrable Darkness, and yet I knew It was the very essence of Light itself.

4. I knew myself to be *beyond space, time, and causality*. As the substantial, spatial, and transcendent 'I', I knew that I sustained the whole phenomenal universe, and that time, space, and law are simply the Self-imposed forms whereby I am enabled to apprehend in the relative sense.[13] I, thus, am not dependent upon the space-time manifold, but, on the contrary, that manifold is dependent upon the Self with which I am identical.

5. Closely associated with the foregoing realization there is a feeling of *complete freedom*. I had broken out of the bondage to the space-time manifold and the law-form governing in this manifold. This is largely an affective value, but one which, to me, is of the very highest importance. The quest for me was less a search for bliss than an effort to satisfy a deep yearning for Freedom.

6. There is the sense of *freedom from guilt*. That feeling, which is variously called sense of sin, guilt, or karmic bondage, dropped completely away from me. The bindings of a discrete individuality no longer existed. The accounts were closed and the books balanced in one grand gesture. This came at once as an immediate affective value, but I realized readily the

underlying rationale. As the individual and personal self, I was bound within the space-time field and necessarily incurred the rebound of all actions there, but, as the transcendent Self, I comprehended that field in its entirety, instead of being comprehended by it. So it might be said that all action and its rebounding were contained within ME, but left the Self, with which I am identical, unaffected in its totality.[14]

7. I both felt and knew that, at last, I had found the *solution of the 'wrongness'*, the sensing of which constitutes the underlying driving force of all religion and much philosophical effort. Beneath the surface of life, in the world-field, there is a feeling of loneliness that is not dissipated by objective achievement or human companionship, however great the range and penetration of sympathetic adjustment. Religious and other literature afford abundant testimony that this feeling of solitude is very widely, if not universally, experienced. I am disposed to regard it as the driving motif of the religious quest. In common with others, I felt this solitude and realized that the sense of incompleteness that it engenders forces the individual to accept one or the other of two alternatives. He may accept the solitude and despair of ever attaining a resolution of it, in which case he accepts fundamental pessimism as part and parcel of the very core of his life. But the feeling of incompleteness may drive him on to a hopeful quest for that which will effect its resolution. The more common mystical resolution is a sense of Union with God, wherein a companionship with a transcendent otherness is attained. My own recognition had more the value of a sort of fusion in identity, wherein the self and the otherness entered into an indistinguishable blend. Before the final moment of the transformation I was aware of an otherness, in some sense, that I sought, but after the culminating moment that

otherness vanished in identity. Consequently, I have no real need of the term "God" in my vocabulary. I find it useful, at times, to employ this term in a literary sense, because it suggests certain values I wish to convey. But its significance is psychological rather than metaphysical.

Through the Recognition, I attained a state wherein I could be at rest and contented in the most profound sense. For me, individually, it was not necessary to seek further, to achieve further, nor to express further in order to know full enjoyment. However, there was a blot on the contentment that grew out of the realization of the pain of the many millions who live in this world, and also out of the knowledge that a private solution of a problem is only a part of the great problem of the philosopher, which is the attainment of a general solution that shall be of the widest possible universality and availability. But all this is not a defect in the adequacy of the transformed state of consciousness itself.

8. There is a decided increase in the realization of the affective qualities of *calmness* and *serenity*. In the immediate presence of the transcendent state the disturbing factors produced by the circumstances and forces of the world-field lose their effective potency. They are simply dissolved away as something irrelevant, or as something that acts so far below one as to leave him in his real being untouched. When in the mystical state, there is no need for trying to be calm and serene, but rather these qualities envelop the individual without his putting forth any specific effort. Subsequently, when I have been out of the immediate presence of the state, it has been easier for me to remain calm and serene than formerly, though the more I am out of the state, the greater is the effort required to retain these affective qualities.

9. The *significance and value of information is radically changed.* Formerly, I acquired information very largely as part of the search for the Real. In the transcendent state I felt myself to be grounded in the Real, in a sense of the utmost intimacy, and since then I have continued to feel this grounding, though involving sometimes less and sometimes more the sense of immediate Presence. At the present time, knowledge, in the sense of information, has value chiefly as an instrument of expression or a means to render manifest that which is already known to me in the most significant sense. This making manifest is valuable, not alone for the reaching of other individuals but likewise for the enriching of my own personal consciousness. The abstract and superconceptual knowing attains a formal and experiential clarification through giving it concrete embodiment in thought. Nevertheless, in all this, knowledge-as-information serves only a secondary role, quite inferior to the vital importance it formerly had. It seems as though, in an unseen and dark sense, I already know all that is to be known. If I so choose, I can give a portion of this knowledge manifested form so that it is revealed to the consciousness of others, as well as to my own personal consciousness. But there is no inner necessity, at least not one of which I am conscious, that drives me on to express and make manifest. I feel quite free to choose such course as I please.

10. The most marked affective quality precipitated within the relative consciousness is that of *felicity*. Joy is realized as a very definite experience. It is of a quality more intense and satisfying than that afforded by any of the experiences or achievements that I have known within the world-field. It is not easy to describe this state of felicity. It is in no sense orgiastic or violent in its nature; on the contrary it is quite subtle, though

highly potent. All world-pleasures are coarse and repellent by contrast. All enjoyment—using this term in the Indian sense—whether of a pleasurable or painful type, I found to be more or less distasteful by contrast. In particular, it is just as completely different from the pleasures experienced through vice as it is possible to imagine. The latter are foiled by a sense of guilt, and this guilt persists long after the pleasure-quality of the vicious experience has passed. The higher felicity seems almost, if not quite, identical with virtue itself. I find myself disposed to agree with Spinoza and say that real felicity is not simply the reward of virtue, but *is* virtue. One feels that there is nothing more right or more righteous, for that matter, than to be so harmonized in one's consciousness as to feel the Joy at all times. It is a dynamic sort of Joy that seems to dissolve such pain as may be in the vicinity of the one who realizes it. This Joy enriches rather than impoverishes others.

I doubt that anyone could possibly appreciate the tremendous value of this felicity without directly experiencing it. I felt, and feel, that no cost could be too high as the price of its attainment, and I find that this testimony is repeated over and over again in mystical literature. It seems as though but a brief experience of this Joy would be worth any effort and any amount of suffering that could be packed into a lifetime that might prove necessary for its realization. I understand now why so much of mystical expression is in the form of rhapsody. It requires an active restraint to avoid the overuse of superlatives, especially as one realizes that all superlatives, as they are understood in the ordinary range of experience, are, in fact, understatements. The flowery expressions of the Persian and Indian mystics are not at all overstatements. But this mode of expression is subject to the weakness that it suggests to the nonmystical reader a loss of critical perspective upon the part of the mystical writer. It is even quite possible to be abandoned in the Joy, and so a real meaning does attach to the idea of "God intoxication." On the whole, it seems probable that the most extreme experience of this Joy is realized by those in whom the affective side of their nature is most developed. If the cognitive interest is of comparable or of superior development, it seems likely that we would find more of the restraint that was evident in men like Spinoza and Buddha.

The Joy seems to be a dynamic force. If one is justified in saying there is such a thing as experiencing force, in the ordinary sense of 'experience', then it certainly is true that one experiences a force either associated with, or identical with, the Joy derived from the transcendental level. In my experience, the nearest analogy is that afforded by a feeling of force I have sometimes experienced in the vicinity of a powerful electric generator.[15] There is something about it that suggests a 'flowing through', though it is impossible to determine any direction of flow, in terms of our ordinary spatial relationships. It induces a sense of physiological, as well as emotional and intellectual, well-being. The sheer joy in life of a healthy youth, who is untroubled by problems, faintly suggests a phase of this sense of well-being. It gives a glow to life and casts a sort of sheath over the environment that tends toward an effect of beauty which at times is very strong. I have demonstrated to my satisfaction that this joyous force, or whatever else it may be called, is capable of being induced, in some measure, in those who may be in the vicinity. I find there are some who will report feeling the joyous quality, even though the state I might be experiencing was not announced or otherwise noted. It is not inconceivable that in this 'force' we are dealing with something that may be within the range of detection by some subtle instrument. Clearly there are detectable physiological effects. Nervous tensions are reduced and the desire for ordinary physical food decreases. In fact, one does have a curious sense of feeling nourished. On the other hand, there are some after effects that suggest that one's organism has been subjected to the action of an energetic field of too intense or high an order for the nervous organism to endure easily. For my part, during the past eight months I have experienced frequent alterations between being in this "force-field" and being more or less completely out of it. The latter I have come to regard as a sort of deflated state. Particularly in the early days and after periods when the 'force' and joy qualities had been especially intense, I found that in the subsequent deflated states there was a subtle sense of fatigue throughout the whole body. Return of the joyous state would at once induce the feeling of well-being. However, I soon realized that a due regard for the capacities of the physical organism rendered necessary a discriminating restraint when inducing the joyous 'force-field'. I found that this 'force' was subject to the will in its personal manifestation and could be held within the limits of intensity to which the organism could adapt itself. In the process of time it does seem that my organism is undergoing a progressive adjustment to the higher energy level.

There are times when this 'force' seems to be of the nature of a flame with which I am identical.[16] In general, this flame is not accompanied with a sense of heat, but under certain conditions it is. Thus, if, while in the 'force-field', I permit myself to feel disturbing affections, I begin to feel heat in the organism. The effect is of such a nature as to suggest that the affective disturbance has a value analogous to resistance in an

electric circuit. It is well known that an electric con-
ductor of sufficiently high resistance will produce heat,
and so the analogy is readily suggested. Further, the
'force-field' does seem, at times, to produce a feeling
of heat in others who are in the vicinity. These are
objective effects, apparently well within the range of
objective determination. Yet, the inciting cause is a
state of consciousness that I find to be subject, in considerable degree, to conscious control through the intervention of purely mental control with no manual
aids. Does this not confirm the suggestion of William
James that there is such a thing as a penetration of
energy into the objective field of consciousness from
other zones of consciousness that are ordinarily in disparate relationship?

Though the symbols of the electromagnetic field
and of fire go far in indicating the quality of this subtle
and joy-giving 'force', they fall short of full adequacy.
The 'force', at the same time, seems to be of fluidic
character. There is something in it like breath and like
water. At this point it is necessary in some measure to
turn away from the mental habits of the modern
chemist and physiologist and try to feel a meaning
closer to that given by the ancients. It is important
that the 'water' should not be thought of as simply
H_2O, and the breath as merely a pulmonary rhythm
involving the inhalation and exhalation of air. In the
present sense, the essence of the water and air lies in
their being life-giving and life-sustaining fluids. The
chemical and physical properties of these fluids are
mere external incidents. In a sense that still remains a
mystery to science, these fluids are vitally necessary to
life. The joy-giving 'force' is Life, but it is life in some
general and universal sense of which life-as-living-
organism is a temporary modification. Thus, to be
consciously identical with this 'force' is to be con-

sciously identical with Life as a principle. It gives a feeling of being alive, beside which the ordinary feeling of life is no more than a mere shadow. And just as the shadow life is obviously mortal, the higher Life is as clearly deathless. It may be said that time is the child of Life in the transcendent sense, while life-as-living organism is the creature of time. Right in this distinction lies one resolution of the whole problem of immortality. So long as the problem is stated in terms of life-as-living-organism, immortality remains inconceivable. In fact, in this sense, all life is no more than a "birthing"-dying flux with no real continuity or duration at all. But the higher Life is identical with duration itself. Hence, he who has consciously realized himself as identical with the higher Life has at the same time become consciously identical with duration. Thus, death-as-termination becomes unthinkable, but, equally, birth is no beginning.

11. There is also associated with the deep feeling of Joy a quality of *Benevolence*. It seems as though the usual self-interest, which tends to be highly developed in the midst of the struggles of objective life, spontaneously undergoes a weakening in force. It is not so much a feeling of active altruism as a being grounded in a kind of consciousness in which the conflict between self-interest and altruism is dissolved. It is more a feeling of interest in good being achieved than simply that I, as an individual, should realize the good. Before the attainment of the Recognition I felt a distinct desire for the attainment of good as something that I, individually, might realize, but once I became identified in consciousness with the transcendent state, the individually self-centered motivation began to weaken. It is as though there is a spreading out of interest so that attainment on the part of any self is my concern as truly as my own individual attainment had

been. There is not the usual sense of self-sacrifice in this, but, rather, a growing impersonality of outlook. In such a state of consciousness one could readily accept a course of action that would involve personal hardship, if only it would serve the purpose of bringing the realization more generally within the range of attainment. It is not a motivation in which the thought of heroism, nobility, or reward plays any part. It simply seems to be the appropriate and sensible course to follow if circumstances indicate that it is necessary. All this is a spontaneous affective state born out of the very nature of the consciousness itself, without thought of an ethical imperative. In the more deflated states of consciousness, I find the force of the feeling considerably weakened, and then it becomes necessary to translate it into the form of a moral imperative to set up a resistance to the old egoistic habits. But on the higher level the moral imperative is replaced by a spontaneous tendency that, when viewed from the relative standpoint, would be called benevolent.

The underlying rationale of this induced attitude seems clear to me. When the 'I' is realized as a sort of universal or 'spatial' Self, synthesizing all selves, the distinction between the 'me' and the 'thou' simply becomes irrelevant. Thus the good of one self is part and parcel with the good of all selves. Consequently, altruism and self-interest come to mean essentially the same thing.[17]

12. Associated with the transcendent Life-force there is a very curious kind of *cognition*. It is not the more familiar analytic kind of intellection. To me this development has proved to be of especial interest, for by temperament and training my mental action, heretofore, has been predominantly analytic. Now analysis achieves its results through a laborious and painful dis-

section of given raw material from experience and a reintegration by means of *invented* concepts applied hypothetically. This gives only external relations and definitely involves 'distance' between the concept and the object it denotes. But there is another kind of intellection in which the concept is born spontaneously and has a curious identity with its object. The Life-force either brings to birth in the mind the concepts without conscious intellectual labor or moves in parallelism with such birth. Subsequently, when these concepts are viewed analytically and critically, I find them almost invariably peculiarly correct. In fact, they generally suggest correlations that are remarkably clarifying and have enabled me to check my insight with the recognition of others.

Undoubtedly, this cognitive process is a phase of what has been called by many 'intuition'. For my part, however, I do not find this term wholly satisfactory, because 'intuition' has been given a number of meanings that are not applicable to this kind of cognition. Accordingly, I have invented a term that seems much more satisfactory. I call it '*Knowledge through Identity*'. As it is immediate knowledge, it is intuitive in the broad sense, but as it is highly noetic, it is to be distinguished from other forms of immediate awareness that are largely, if not wholly, noncognitive. There are intuitive types of awareness that are quite alogical, and, therefore such that they do not lead to logical development from out their own nature. In contrast, Knowledge through Identity is potentially capable of expansive development of the type characteristic of pure mathematics. Knowledge through Identity may give the fundamental propositions or 'indefinables' from which systems can grow at once by pure deductive process. Knowledge through Identity is not to be regarded as an analytic extraction from experience, but rather as a Knowledge that is original and coextensive with a Recognizable, but nonexperiential, Reality. It is capable of rendering experience intelligible, but is not itself dependent upon experience.

A realization of Knowledge through Identity does not seem to be an invariable, or even usual, consequence of mystical unfoldment. My studies of the record have led me to the tentative conclusion that it occurs in the case of certain types of mystical unfoldment, of which Spinoza, Plotinus, and Shankara afford instances. In such cases the cognitive interest and capacity is peculiarly notable. But the larger class of cases in which the mystical sense is well developed seems to be of quite a different type. The well-known Persian mystics, presumptively the larger number of of the Indian mystics, most of the Christian mystics, and naturalistic mystics such as Whitman seem quite clearly to fall into some other classification or classifications. With all of these the affective consciousness is dominant and the cognitive interest and capacity may be—though not necessarily—but poorly developed. With them, expression is almost wholly in terms of art or way of life, rather than in terms of philosophical systems. Apparently, the noetic quality of their mystical consciousness is quite subordinate to the affective, and in some cases, even to the sensuous, values.

13. *Atypical features.* There are certain respects in which the precipitated effects from the transcendent consciousness, as experienced by me, differ from typical mystical experience. I have not known the so-called automatisms, a class of psychical manifestations that are so commonly reported. My psychical organization does not seem to be of the type requisite for this kind of experience. I have never heard words coming as though uttered on another level of being and having the seeming of objective sound. Even the thought has

not seemed to come from a source extraneous to my-self. I have thought more deeply and more trenchantly than has hitherto been possible for me as personal man, but the sense of intimate union with the thought has been greater than was ever true of the former personal thinking. Never has my thought been less mediumistic. Formerly, my personal thought has often been a reflection of a thought originated by someone else and not fully made my own before I used it. There is a certain kind of mediumship in this, although in this sense practically everybody is a medium part of the time and many all the time. The thought that I have found born in the Recognition is nonmediumistic in the strictest sense, since it is MY thought but more than my *personal* thought.

There never has been at any time a writing through my hand in an automatic sense. What I have written has been my own conscious thought, with full con-sciousness of the problems of word selection and gram-matical construction. The effective words and the cor-rect constructions I find myself able to produce much more easily than formerly, but there is a conscious selective effort required at all times.[18]

When in the field of the 'Life-force,' the action of the understanding is both more profound and more trenchant than when in the 'deflated' state, but the difference is one of degree and not of two radically separated and discontinuous states of consciousness of such a nature that the inferior consciousness is quite incapable of understanding what is written under the guidance of the higher. The inferior phase of con-sciousness, when operating by itself, does not under-stand as easily nor does it have as wide a grasp of the bearings of the thought. But, in some degree, the in-ferior phase readily becomes more or less infused with the superior by the simple application of effort to understand. The effect is analogous to the superposition of two rays of light, with both of which I am identical, the resultant being an intensified consciousness that is at the same time relative and transcendent, in some way that is not wholly clear to introspective analysis.

These states of Recognition have never been associated with the so-called photisms. They most certainly had Light-value, and I frequently have occasion to use the word 'Light' to express an important quality of the higher consciousness, but this is 'Light' as an illuminating force in consciousness and not a sensible light apparently seen as with the eyes. There have been a very few of these so-called photisms when in a kind of dreaming state when half asleep, but these have not occurred at times close to the periods of the deeper Recognitions.

Never have I had experience of the type commonly called psychical clairvoyance. It is possible that the strength of my intellectual interest operates as a barrier to this kind of experience. I admit having an interest in such experience and would consider it a valuable object of study if it came my way. But I would not tolerate such a capacity for experience if the price exacted was a growth of confusion in understanding. On the whole, psychical clairvoyance seems to be quite frequently associated with mystical unfoldment, perhaps more the rule than the exception. There even seems to be some tendency to confuse this clairvoyance with genuine mystical value. However, the two are by no means identical, nor are they necessarily associated.

I have found that there is a very important difference between psychical experience and noetic Recognition. The transcendent Consciousness is highly noetic, but on its own level is quite impersonal. In order that a correlation may be established between the personal consciousness and the transcendental state, there must be an active and conscious intermediating agent. The evidence is that this intermediating agent may be, and apparently generally is, an irrational psyche of which the individual is more or less conscious. But the intermediation may be intellectual with little or no conscious correlation with the irrational psyche. It seems practically certain that the precipitated effects withon the personal consciousness by the two routes should not be congruent in form.

14. If *ecstasy* is to be regarded as a state of consciousness always involving a condition of trance, then that state of consciousness that I have realized and called "transcendental Recognition" is not one of ecstasy. However, there is considerable reason for believing that Ecstasy, or Samadhi—the Indian equivalent—is not necessarily associated with trance. It becomes very largely a question of the basis of classification. If the externally discernible marks or symptoms of a state are to be regarded as determinate, then ecstasy, as ordinarily conceived, is a trance or trance-like condition. But if the inner consciousness-value is to be the ground of classification, then there is excellent evidence that Ecstasy or Samadhi may be realized without trance.[19] The latter basis of classification seems to me to be of far more significance, for the external symptoms of trance mark widely different inner states of consciousness, such as those of hysteria, mediumship, and hypnosis, as well as Ecstasy in the higher sense.

By subsequent comparison it appears that the noetic and consciousness values that I have realized have a very great deal in common with those reported by Plotinus as characteristic of the state of Ecstasy. I find a marked congruency between my present outlook and that given in the teachings of Buddha and in the writing of Shankara. But neither of these men regarded the state of trance as necessary for the realization of the states they called Dhyana or Samadhi, although Buddha seemed to have no objection in principle to the use of trance as a means of attaining the higher state of consciousness. It seems rather clear that the state of the personal organism is a matter of only secondary importance, while other factors are primarily determinant.

For my own part, never in my life have I lost objective consciousness, save in normal sleep. At the time of the Recognition on August 7, I was at all times aware of my physical environment and could move the body freely at will. Further, I did not attempt to stop the activity of the mind, but simply very largely ignored the stream of thought. There was, however, a "fading down" of the objective consciousness, analogous to that of a dimming of a lamp without complete extinguishment. The result was that I was in a sort of compound state wherein I was both here and 'There', with the objective consciousness less acute than normal. It is very probable that the concentrated inward state would have been fuller and more acute had the objective stream of consciousness been stopped entirely as in a trance, but with regard to this I cannot speak from personal experience.[20]

The literature on the subject of mystical states very clearly reveals their transciency. Often the state is only momentary and, it is said, rarely exceeds two hours in duration. Of course, the only phase of such states that affords a basis for time-measurement is that part that overlaps the objective consciousness. The inmost content of the state does not lend itself to time-measurement at all. Its value, therefore, is not a function of time. But if we take the perspective of the personal consciousness, it is possible to isolate a period during which the recognition was more or less full, and this can be measured. In my own experience I am unable to give definite data with respect to this feature. For the first ten days following the awakening I was far too greatly occupied with the contemplation of the values unfolding in my consciousness to think of the question of time-measurement, and in addition, at that time I had not been familiar with psychological studies of the subject and so knew nothing about duration norms. As I look at the whole period retrospectively, I do not see how a very definite time-measurement could have been made. There was a sharply defined moment at which the state was initiated, but there was no moment at which I could say it definitely closed. A series of alternate phases and variable degrees of depth of consciousness are discernible, so that at times I have been more transcendentally conscious and at others less so. A different base of life and valuation has become normal, so that, in one sense, the recognition has remained as a persistent state. Yet there are notable differences of phases.

During the first ten days I was repeatedly in and out, or more in and more out—I am not sure which is the more correct statement—of what I have called the 'Life-force' field. I soon found that the stronger intensity of the field was a real strain upon the organism and so I consciously imposed a certain restraint upon the tendency of the states to deepen until I finally achieved a certain adjustment and adaptation with respect to the nervous organism. After the close of the first ten days it was suggested to me that it would be well to keep a record of the effects of the transformation, and so at that time I began to write and continued to do so for about four months. While the effort at formulation was a little difficult at first, the writing soon acquired momentum, and presently I found ideas developing in my consciousness faster than I could give them expression. During this whole period there were many times when the consciousness was dominantly on the noetic level, with more objective intervals interspersed. At first the range of oscillation was more notable than toward the end. In the course of time, it seems, the personal consciousness has gradually adapted itself to a higher level, so that the periods of inward penetration do not afford the same contrast as formerly. The first period of a little more than one month constitutes a phase that stands out by itself, with a fairly sharp dividing line at its culmination between the eighth and ninth of September. During this time the prime focus of my consciousness was toward the transcendent, while in the subsequent phase, continuing to the present, I have rather taken this transcendent consciousness as a base and focused more toward the relative world. The consequence is that there is a sense in which I look back to those first thirty-odd days as a sort of high point in consciousness, a seed-sowing period, from which various fruitings have followed ever since. Frankly, these thirty-odd days constitute a period that I view as the best I have ever known. Referring to a symbol that Plato has made immortal, I would say that this was a time when I stepped outside the 'cave' and realized directly the glory of the 'sun-illumined' world, after which I turned back again to the life in the 'cave', but with this permanent difference in outlook—that I could never again regard the 'cave life' with the same seriousness that I had once given it. Thus, in this cycle, there is something to be differentiated from all the rest.

During that first month the current of bodily life was definitely weaker than during the preceding and following phases. The desire for sentient existence was decidedly below normal. The spontaneous inclination was all in the direction of the transcendent consciousness. Physical life was clearly a burden, a sort of blinder superimposed upon consciousness. I even felt a distaste for physical food. I am convinced that if I had not supplemented the weakened desire for physical existence by a definite and conscious will-to-live, the body would have started into a decline. I became hypersensitive and found it very difficult to drive an automobile in traffic. I had to exert the will consciously, where formerly I had acted through automatic habit. But on the other hand, I found the will more effective than previously, so I was enabled adequately to replace spontaneous inclination with conscious control. Fortunately, my earlier studies had prepared me for this state of feeling and I knew that I was facing a temptation that others had faced before me. For there is such a thing as a world-duty that remains even after the desire for sentient existence has disappeared. But this did not keep me from thinking how delightful it would be to abandon all to the transcendent consciousness.

Concomitantly with the loss of desire for sentient life there was a growth in the sense of power. I felt I had a certain power of conscious control over forces that ordinarily operate beneath the level of consciousness, and my subsequent experience has tended to confirm this. It is a sort of raw power without the detailed knowledge of how to apply it. In other words, the knowledge of effective practical use had to be developed through experiment. But I have found, very clearly, that I possess a power that formerly I did not know. I can choose and will consciously, where formerly the current of unconscious forces was determinent.

Before the close of the first month the decision to continue as an active factor in the world-field had become definite, despite the distaste I felt for this domain. It felt like turning one's back upon a rich mine of jewels after gathering but a handful, and then marching back into the dreary domain of iron and brass. However, I found that it could be done, and then I accepted what I thought would be a future in which the best would always be a memory. I had found what I sought during many years and could see nothing but anticlimax thereafter, so far as the immediately realized consciousness values were concerned. So the further Recognition, which closed the first cycle, came as a complete surprise, for not only did I not seek it, I did not even know that such a state existed, or if it existed, that it was within the range of human consciousness. I had now already known a state of consciousness that certainly had the value of Liberation. A subsequent search through mystical literature revealed that it was substantially congruent with mystical experience as such and was distinctly more comprehensive than many of the mystical unfoldments. So far as I was familiar with it, the Brahmanical literature always represented the Liberated State as the end-term of all attainment. In this literature I had found nothing requiring more depth of insight than I now had glimpsed, although there was a vast mass of psychic detail quite foreign to my experience. So I was quite unprepared to find that there were even deeper levels of transcendence. However, had I understood a few obscure references in Buddhist literature I would have been warned.

In order to reach some understanding of the culminating phase of the Recognition, certain contrasting facts concerning the first phase must be given emphasis. As I have already affirmed, there is sufficient evidence of the fact of mystical recognition, together with reported affective value, to render it an object of possible desire. Long ago I had learned enough to realize that it was desirable and had set forth in search of it. There also exists a sufficient statement of the reasons why an individual who has attained this Recognition should turn his back upon it, as it were, to show that such a course was desirable in its social bearings. But there does not seem to be anything further that could be conceived as an object of desire. Now, the culminating effect of the present Realization with respect to desire is that the latter has fulfilled its office in the individual sense, and there is nothing more to wish for. I certainly felt in the transcendent state abundant completion and vastly more than I had anticipated. So, what more could there be?

I see now that there was a defect in this completion that kept it from being a full state of equilibrium. It consisted preeminently of the positive end-terms of the best in human consciousness. Thus it was a state of superlative Joy, Peace, Rest, Freedom, and Knowledge; and all this stands in contrast to the world-field as fullness contrasts to emptiness.[21] Hence there did exist a tension in the sense of attractiveness that was incompatible with the perfection of balance. There was a distinction between being bound to embodied consciousness and not being so bound that made a difference to me. I had to resist the inclination toward the latter state in order to continue existence in the former. In other words, there are in this earlier phase of Recognition certain tensions that call for a higher resolution. But it was the perspective of the culminating Recognition that rendered all of this clear. The first stage did not, of itself, disclose any further possibility of conceivable attainment, and so I was disposed to give it a greater terminal value than it really possessed.

So far I have outlined three progressively comprehensive Recognitions. Each was realized after a period of conscious effort in the appropriate direction. In each case I had some reason to believe that there was a goal to be sought. In the first two instances I was aware that there was something more remaining to be realized, because the sense of incompleteness was only partly liquidated. In the third instance this liquidation seemed to be complete, and then I simply turned my back upon the full individual enjoyment of it for such period of time as might be necessary to fulfill some more comprehensive purpose reaching beyond individual concerns. In contrast, the culminating Recognition came with the force of an unexpected bestowal without my having put forth any conscious personal effort toward the attainment of it. Thus, in this case, my personal relationship or attitude was passive in a deep sense.

During the day preceding the final Recognition I had been busy writing and my mind was exceptionally clear and acute. In fact, the intellectual energy was of an unusual degree of intensity. The mood was decidedly one of intellectual assertion and dominance. This feature is interesting for the reason that it is precisely the state of mind that ordinarily would be regarded as least favorable for the 'breaking through' to mystical modes of consciousness. The rule seems to be that the thought must be silenced or at least reduced in intensity and ignored in the meditation.[22] In the records of mystical awakening it is almost always made evident that preceding the state of Illumination there is at least a brief period of quiescence of conscious activity. Sometimes this appears as though there were a momentary standing still of all nature. For my part I had previously been aware of a kind of antecedent stillness before each of the critical moments, though it was not translated as stillness of nature. But in the case of the fourth Recognition, the foreground was one of intense mental tension and exceptional intellectual activity. It was not now a question of capturing something of extreme subtlety that might be dispersed by a breath of mental or affective activity. It was more a case of facing an overwhelming power that required all the active phase of the resources of consciousness to face it.

The Event came after retiring. I became aware of a deepening effect in consciousness that presently acquired or manifested a dominant affective quality. It was a state of utter Satisfaction. But here there enters a strange and almost weird feature. Language, considered as standing in a representative relationship to something other than the terms of the language, ceased to have any validity at this level of consciousness. In a sense, the words and that which they mean are interblended in a kind of identity. Abstract ideas cease to be artificial derivatives from a particularized experience, but are transformed into a sort of universal substantiality. The relative theories of knowledge simply do not apply at this level. So 'Satisfaction' and the *state* of satisfaction possess a substantial and largely inexpressible identity. Further, this 'Satisfaction', along with its substantiality, possesses a universal character. It is the value of all possible satisfactions at once and yet like a "thick" substance interpenetrating everywhere. I know how weird this effort at formulation must sound, but unless I abandon the attempt to interpret, I must constrain language to serve a purpose quite outside normal usage.[23]

This state of 'Satisfaction' is a kind of integration of all previous values. It is the culminating fulfillment of all desires and thus renders the desire-tension, as such, impossible. One can desire only when there is in some sense a lack, an incompleteness, that needs to be fulfilled, or a sensed goal that remains to be attained.

When in every conceivable or felt sense all is attained, desire simply has to drop out.[24] The result is a profound balance in consciousness, a state of thorough repose with no drawing or inclining in any direction. Hence, in the sum total, such a state is passive. Now, while this state is, in one sense, an integration of previous values, it also proved preliminary to a still deeper state. Gradually the 'Satisfaction' faded into the background and by insensible gradation became transformed into a state of 'Indifference'.[25] For while satisfaction carries the fullness of active affective and conative value, indifference is really affective-conative silence. It is the superior terminus of the affective-conative mode of human consciousness. There is another kind of indifference where this mode of consciousness has bogged down into a kind of death. This is to be found in deeply depressed states of human consciousness. The 'High Indifference', however, is the superior or opposite pole beyond which motivation and feeling in the familiar human sense cannot reach. But, most emphatically, it is not a state of reduced life or consciousness.[26] On the contrary, it is both life and consciousness of an order of superiority quite beyond imagination. The concepts of relative consciousness simply cannot bound it. In one sense, it is a terminal state, but at the same time, in another sense, it is initial. Everything can be predicated of it so long as the predication is not privative, for in the privative sense nothing can be predicated of it. It is at once rest and action, and the same may be said with respect to all other polar qualities. I know of only one concept that would suggest its noetic value as a whole, and this is the concept of 'Equilibrium', yet even this is a concession to the needs of relative thinking. It is both the culmination and beginning of all possibilities.

In contrast with the preceding Recognition, this

state is not characterized by an intensive or active feeling of felicity. It could be called blissful only in the sense that there is an absence of all pain in any respect whatsoever. But I felt myself to be on a level of consciousness where there is no need of an active joy. Felicity, together with all other qualities, is part of the blended whole and by the appropriate focusing of individual attention can be isolated from the rest and thus actively realized, if one so desired. But for me there seemed to be no need of such isolation. The consciousness was so utterly whole that it was unnecessary to administer any affective quality to give it a greater richness. I was superior to all affective modes, as such, and thus could command and manifest any of them that I might choose. I could bless with beneficent qualities or impose the negative ones as a curse. Still the state itself was too thoroughly void of the element of desire for me to feel any reason why I should bless or curse. For within that perfection there is no need for any augmentation or diminution.

While within this state I recalled the basis of my previous motivation and realized that if this state had been outlined to me then as an abstract idea, it could not by any possibility have seemed attractive. But while fused with the state, all other states that could formerly have been objects of desire seemed flaccid by comparison. The highest conceivable human aspiration envisages a goal inevitably marred by the defects of immature imagination. Unavoidably, to the relative consciousness the complete balance of the perfect consciousness must seem like a void, and thus the negation of every conceivable possible value. But to be identified with this supernal State implies abandonment of the very base of relative consciousness, and thus is a transcendence of all relative valuation. To reach back to that relative base involves a contraction and blinding of consciousness, an acceptance of an immeasurable lessness. In the months following the Recognition, when I had once again resumed the drama in the relative field, I have looked back to that Transcendent State as to a consciousness of a most superior and desirable excellence. All other values have become thin and shallow by contrast. Nevertheless I carry with me always the memory, and more than a memory, of the immediate knowledge of it, and this is something quite different from a mediately conveyed and abstract portrayal of it as a merely possible consciousness.

As an intimate part of that supernal consciousness, there is a sense of power and authority literally of cosmic proportions.[27] By contrast, the marchings of the Caesars and the conquests of science are but the games of children. For these achievements, which seem so portentous and commanding upon the pages of human history, all inhere in a field of consciousness that in its very roots is subject to that Higher Power and Authority. Before mere cataclysms of nature, if they are on sufficiently large a scale, the resources of our mightiest rulers and of our science stand impotent. Yet those very forces of nature rest dependent upon that transcendent and seeming Void in order that they may have any existence whatsoever. The mystery before birth and after death lies encompassed within it. All this, all this play of visible and invisible forces seem no more than a dream-drama during a moment's sleep in the illimitable vastness of Eternity. And so, from out that Eternity speaks the Voice of the never-sleeping Consciousness, and before the commanding Authority and irresistible Power of that Voice, all dreams, though of cosmic proportions, dissolve.

Now, as I write, there returns once again an adumbrative Presence of that awful Majesty. This time, as I am focused upon the problem of objective formulation, I am less blended in the Identity, and sense IT as 'Presence'. This mind, which once carved its way through the mysteries of the functions of the complex variable and the Kantian transcendental deduction of the categories, fairly trembles at its daring to apprehend THAT which threatens momentarily to dissolve the very power of apprehension itself. Fain would the intellect retreat into the pregnant and all-encompassing Silence, where the 'Word-without-form' alone is true. This personal being trembles upon the brink of the illimitable Abyss of irrelevance that dissolves inevitably the mightiest worlds and suns. But there remains a task to be done and there may be no disembarking yet.

At the time of the culminating Recognition I found myself spreading everywhere and identical with a kind of "Space" that embraced not merely the visible forms and worlds, but all modes and qualities of consciousness as well. However, all these are not There as disparate and objective existences; they are blended, as it were, in a sort of primordial and culminating totality. It seemed that the various aspects and modes that are revealed to the analysis of relative consciousness could have been projected into differentiated manifestation, if I chose so to will it, but all such projection would have left unaffected the perfect balance of that totality, and whether or not the projecting effort was made was completely a matter of indifference. That totality was, and is, not other than myself, so that the study of things and qualities was resolved into simple self-examination. Yet it would be a mistake to regard the state as purely subjective. The preceding Recognition had been definitely a subjective penetration, and during the following month I found myself inwardly polarized to an exceptional degree. In contrast, the final Recognition seemed like a movement in consciousness toward objectivity, but not in the sense of a movement toward the relative world-field. The final State is, at once, as much objective as subjective, and also as much a state of action as of rest. But since it is all coexistent on a timeless level, the objectivity is not discrete and differentiated, and consequently is quite unlike the relative world. The Godless secular universe vanishes, and in its place there remains none other than the living and all-enveloping Presence of Divinity itself. So, speaking in the subjective sense, I am all there is, yet at the same time, objectively considered, there is nought but Divinity spreading everywhere. Thus the level of the High Indifference may be regarded as the terminal Value reached by delving into that which, in the relative world, man calls his 'I', and yet, equally, the final culmination of all that appears objective. But this objectivity, in the final sense, is simply pure Divinity. So the sublimated object and the sublimated self are one and the same Reality, and this may be represented by the judgment: "I am the Divinity."[28] The Self is not of inferior dignity to the Divine, nor that Divinity subordinate to the Self. And it is only through the realization of this equality that it is possible for the individual to retain his integration before that tremendous all-encompassing Presence. In any case, the dissolving force is stupendous, and there is no inclination to resist it.

Throughout the whole period of this supreme state of consciousness I was self-consciously awake in the physical body and quite aware of my environment. The thought-activity was not depressed, but on the contrary, alert and acute. I was continuously conscious of my self-identity, in two distinct senses. In one sense, I was, and am, the primordial Self and co-terminous with an unlimited and abstract Space, while at the same time the subject-object and self-analyzing consciousness was a sort of point-presence within that Space. An illustration is afforded by thinking of the former as being of the nature of an original Light, in itself substantial, spreading throughout, but not derived from any center, while the latter is a point-centered and reflected light, such as that of a searchlight. The searchlight of the self-analyzing consciousness can be directed anywhere within the primordial Light, and thus serves to render chosen zones self-conscious. Through the latter process I was enabled to capture values within the framework of the relative consciousness and thus am enabled to remember not merely a dimly sensed fact of an inchoate transcendence but, as well, all that I am now writing and a vastly more significant conscious integration that defeats all efforts at formulation. The primordial consciousness is timeless, but the self-analyzing action was a process occurring in time. And so that part that I have been enabled to carry with me in the relative state is just so much as I could think into the mind during the interval of penetration. Naturally, I centered my attention on the features that to me as an individual appeared to be of the greater significance.

It seems to me that this that I have called the Primordial Consciousness must be identical with von Hartmann's 'Unconscious'. For what is the difference between 'consciousness' and 'unconsciousness' if there is no self-consciousness present? Sheer consciousness that is not aware of itself, by reason of that very fact, would not know that it was conscious. Thus, an individual who has never known ill health or pain remains largely unconscious of his organism. But with the coming of pain he is at once aware of that organism in a sense that was not true before. Then, later, with the passing of the pain, particularly if it has been of protracted duration, he becomes conscious of well-being in his organism. Well-being has taken on a new conscious value. It is at once suggested that self-consciousness is aroused through resistance in some sense, an interference with the free flow of the stream of consciousness. When this occurs, a distinction between consciousness and unconsciousness is produced that had no meaning before. Now this line of reflection has suggested to me that the real distinction should not be made between consciousness and unconsciousness but rather between self-consciousness and the absence of self-consciousness. When there is no self-consciousness in a given zone there is then no more valid basis for predicating sheer unconsciousness than there is for saying that it is a zone of consciousness that is not self-conscious. On the basis of such a view, would not the problem of interpreting how the so-called 'unconscious' enters into consciousness become greatly simplified?

The Primordial Consciousness cannot be described as conceptual, affective, or perceptual. It seems that all these functions are potentially There, but the Consciousness as a whole is a blend of all these and something more. It is a deep, substantial, and vital sort of consciousness, the matter, form, and awareness functions of consciousness all at once. It is not a consciousness or knowledge 'about', and thus is not a field of relationships. The substantiality and the consiousness do not exist as two separable actualities, but rather it would be more nearly correct to say that the consciousness is substance and the substance is consciousness, and thus that these are two interpenetrating modes of the whole. It is certainly a richly 'thick' consciousness and quite other than an absolutely "thin" series of terms in relation.[29]

While in the State I was particularly impressed with the fact that the logical principle of contradiction simply had no relevancy. It would not be correct to say that this principle was violated, but rather, that it had no application. For to isolate any phase of the State was to be immediately aware of the opposite phase as the necessary complementary part of the first. Thus the attempt of self-conscious thought to isolate anything resulted in the immediate initiation of a sort of flow in the very essence of consciousness itself, so that the nascent isolation was transformed into its opposite as copartner in a timeless reality. Every attempt I made to capture the State within the categories of relative knowledge was defeated by this flow effect. Yet there was no sense of being in a strange world. I have never known another state of consciousness that seemed so natural, normal, and proper. I seemed to know that this was the nature that Reality must possess, and somehow, I had always known it. It rather seemed strange that for so many years I had been self-conscious in another form and imagined myself a stranger to this. It seemed to be the real underlying fact of all consciousness of all creatures.

I remembered my former belief in the reality of suffering in the world. It had no more force than the memory of a dream. I saw that, in reality, there is no suffering anywhere, that there is no creature in need of an aiding hand. The essential consciousness and life of all beings are already in that State, and both never had been, and could not be, divorced from it. The world-field with all its striving and pain, seemingly lasting through billions of years, actually is, or seems to be, a dream occurring during a passing wink of sleep. I simply could not feel any need or duty that would call me back to action in the world-field. There was no question of departing from or deserting anybody or any duty, for I found myself so identical with all, that the last most infinitesimal element of distance was dissolved. I remembered that it had been said that there were offices of compassion to be performed in the world, but this idea had no reality in the State because none there was or ever could be who had need for ought, although those who were playing with the dream of life in form might delude themselves with imagining that a need existed. But I knew there was no reality in this dream.[30]

The imperative of the moral law no longer existed, for there was not, and is not, either good or evil. It seemed I could invoke power, even in potentially unlimited degree. I could choose action or rest. If I acted, then I could proceed in any direction I might select. Yet, whether I acted or did not act, or whether I acted in one way or another, it all had absolutely the same significance. It was neither right nor wrong to choose anything, or putting it otherwise, there was neither merit nor demerit in any choice. It was as though any choice whatsoever became immediately Divinely ordained and superior to the review of any lesser tribunal.

To me, individually, the State was supremely attractive, and as the period continued, I seemed to be rising into an irrevocable blending with it. I recalled that if in the self-conscious sense I never returned from this State there would be some in this world who would miss me and would seem, in their relative consciousness, to suffer. Yet it was only with effort that I could give this thought any effective force. For many years I had known from my studies that reports existed of realizable states of consciousness such that the relative state could be completely and finally abandoned. I had also been impressed with the teaching that it was a wiser course to resist that tendency and hold correlation with the relative form of consciousness. I had been convinced by the reasoning supporting the latter course and had for some time resolved to follow it, if ever the opportunity to choose came to me. This doubtless established a habit-form in the personal consciousness, and so far as I can see, that habit alone, or at least mainly, was the decisive factor. For while in the State there simply is no basis for forming any kind of decision, unless that ground is already well established in the individual consciousness out of the life that has gone before. As a result, there was a real conflict between the attraction the State had for me, as a center of individual consciousness, and the impress of the earlier-formed choice, but *I*, in my inmost nature, was not a party to this conflict, rather standing back indifferent to the outcome, knowing quite well that any outcome was Divinely right. The issue seemed to be a closely drawn one, for as time went on—from the relative standpoint—the organized man appeared to be vanishing, but not in the sense of the disappearance of a visually apparent object. It was more a vanishing as irrelevance may cause an issue or a consideration to disappear. It was as though Space were progressively consuming the whole personal and thinking entity in a wholeness-comprehension, beside which all particularities are as nought. Personally, I seemed powerless in the process, not because I lacked command of potential power, but simply because there was no reason—no desire—for rendering the potential kinetic. In the end, I fell asleep, to awaken the next morning in full command of my relative faculties; and clearly the issue had been decided. Was it a victory? From certain points of view, yes. Yet, as I recall the profounder State of Consciousness, which has continued ever since to seem close in the deeper recesses of my private consciousness, I cannot say that in the ultimate sense there was either victory or defeat. The choice was right, *for no choice could possibly be wrong.*

The full cycle of this final Recognition lasted for some hours, with the self-consciousness alert throughout the period. But the depth of the State developed progressively, and at the final stage entered a peculiarly significant phase that strained my self-conscious resources to the utmost. There finally arrived a stage wherein both that which I have called the Self and that which had the value of Divinity were dissolved in a Somewhat, still more transcendent. There now remained nought but pure Being that could be called neither the Self nor God. No longer was "I" spreading everywhere through the whole of an illimitable and conscious Space, nor was there a Divine Presence all about me, but everywhere only Consciousness with no subjective nor objective element. Here, both symbols and concepts fail. But now I know that within and surrounding all there is a Core or Matrix within which are rooted all selves and all Gods, and that from this lofty Peak, veiled in the mists of timeless obscurity and surrounded by thick, impenetrable Silence, all worlds and beings, all spaces and all times lie suspended in utter dependence. On that highest Peak I could Know no more, for the Deeps of the deepest Darkness, and the SILENCE enshrouded in manifold sheaths of Silence rolled over me, and self-consciousness was blown out. But o'er this I heard as the faintest shadow of a breath of consciousness a Voice, as it were, from out a still vaster BEYOND.

There remain to be considered the effects of these Recognitions upon me as an individual center of consciousness, thinking, feeling, and acting within the relative world. Of course, in this, my own statement is necessarily incomplete, since it is confined to an introspective analysis, and lacks the objective valuation that only a witness could supply. But it can render explicit that which no one else could know, since it reveals, as far as it goes, the immediate conscious values.

The Recognition of September 8 and 9 initiated a radical change of phase in the individual consciousness, as compared to the cycle of the preceding month. As already noted, the latter was very largely an indrawn state of consciousness, and the physical organism tended to become overly sensitive to the conditions of physical life. It was more difficult than it had been to meet the ordinary problems arising from the circumstances of the environment. The tumultuous forces of the modern city seemed far too violent to be endured. Even though living in the relative isolation of a suburban community, there still remained the irritations of a mechanical age and subtle impingements of a nature very hard to define. My natural inclination was to seek the wilds where the competitions of objective life-pressures would be at a minimum. It was a real problem of endurance. In contrast, after the final Recognition I noted a distinct growth of organic ruggedness. And, although I have never come to enjoy the harsh dissonances and regimented existence of modern town life, yet I find I have a definitely increased strength for the making of the various needed adjustments. There is an increased capacity to assert command with respect to the various environmental factors. I seem to have the capacity to will embodied existence, regardless of inclination.

On the intellectual side, I have noted a definite revitalization. I have found myself able to sustain creative and analytic thought activity at a higher level than formerly and for longer periods of time. Difficult concepts have become easier of comprehension. The seeming aging effect in the mind, that had been troubling me for sometime, passed, and in its place there came a very definite increase of intellectual vitality; and this has remained to the present hour as a persistent asset.

The affective changes are in the direction of a greater degree of impersonality. There is certainly less personal emotional dependence, and as far as I can detect, a practical unconsciousness of anything like personal slights, if there has been anything of that sort. I do care deeply for the growth of durable well-being, especially for those who come within my orbit, but also in the sense of a general social growth. Yet I find myself considerably indifferent to, when not disgusted with, the rather trivial foibles that make up so large a part of the day-to-day life of most human beings. I am not yet superior to the feeling of indignation, but this feeling is mainly aroused when noting the rapid growth of wilful and violent irrationalism, which has so rapidly engulfed most of the present world. However, I recognize this as a defect due to insufficient personal detachment. For, philosophically, I do realize that men have the right to learn the lessons that folly has to teach, and it is but natural that a certain class of leaders should make capital of this fact. Still, it remains hard to reconcile current morally decadent tendencies with the decades and centuries of relative enlightenment that have been so recent. I find that I had had too high an opinion of the intelligence of the average man, and that the individual who is capable of understanding the wisdom contained in the fable of the goose that laid the golden egg is really quite above the average level of intelligence. Frankly, I have not yet completely adjusted myself to the disillusionment that comes with a more objective and realistic appreciation of what the average human being is, when considered as a relative entity. This comes partly from an increased clarification of insight, and while I am much more certainly aware of the Jewel hidden within the mud of the personal man, yet I see more clearly also the fact of the mud and its unwholesome composition. It is not a pretty sight and not such as to increase one's regard for this world-field. All in all, the more objective my understanding of the actualities of this relative life, the more attractive the Transcendent World becomes.

Probably the most important permanent effect of the whole group of Recognitions is the grounding of knowledge, affection, and the sense of assurance on a base that is neither empirical nor intellectual. This base is supersensible, superaffective, and superconceptual, yet it is both conscious and substantial and of unlimited dynamic potentiality. I feel myself closer to universals than to the particulars given through experience, the latter occupying an essentially derivative position and being only of instrumental value, significant solely as implements for the arousing of self-consciousness. As a consequence, my ultimate philosophic outlook cannot be comprehended within the forms that assume time, the subject-object relationship, and experience as original and irreducible constants of consciousness or reality. At the same time, although I find the Self to be an element of consciousness of more fundamental importance than the foregoing three, yet in the end it, also, is reduced to a derivative position in a more ultimate Reality. So my outlook must deviate from those forms of Idealism that represent the Self as the final Reality. In certain fundamental respects, at least, the formulation must accord with the anatmic doctrine of Buddha, and therefore differ in important respects from any extant western system.[31]

1. In the symbolical language so commonly employed for portraying the stages on the Way, this "critical point" is represented by the desert symbolism. The field of consciousness is watered by the stream of libido (the term of analytic psychology), and when this stream is turned off, the garden or jungle that filled that field withers, leaving a desert. Between the turning off of the libido-stream and its subsequent breakthrough on another course, there is a lapse of more or less time, or at least so I found it. The resultant state is one of aridity with no interest anywhere. Mystical literature is full of references to this stage.

2. At this stage, encouragement from a Sage whom I knew was an important, perhaps decisive, help. But while this Sage encouraged and stimulated flagging interest, he would not tell me what to do, leaving me to my own devices.

3. In the contrast between the theoretical acceptance and the Recognition, I did not find any addition or diminution of thinkable content. But in the case of the recognition, the effect upon the mind was something like an insemination —a vitalizing force. In addition to the unseen, inward deepening of value, there was an objective effect, in that the thought flowed more spontaneously, more acutely, and with much greater assurance. The thought developed of itself, in high degree, without the sense of conscious labor. At the same time I *knew* the truth of the thought and did not merely *believe* in it. Yet, everything that I could think and say might very well have been worked out by the ordinary methods of conscious intellectual labor. But in the later case the sense of assurance is lacking, as well as the sense of supernal value. With these recognitions there is, in addition to the transcendental values, a genuine rejuvenation and vitalization of the mind. This fact became extremely notable at the time of the later radical transformation.

4. The doctrine of the nonexistence of the atman. This is equivalent to the denial of the reality of the self, either in the sense of the personal ego or in that more comprehensive sense of denial of substantive self-existence of the subject, whether pragmatic or transcendental.

5. About two months prior to the 'breakthrough,' while

occupied with a course of lectures in a middle western city, I experienced a three-week period of heavy drowsiness. Except when actually on the platform, I desired to sleep practically all the time. I simply had to give way to this inclination a good many hours of each day, but it did not seem that I could ever get enough sleep. The condition broke very suddenly, and then my mind became more alert than it had been for some years. I was aware of the great inner excitement and somehow seemed to know that I was near the day of final success. In later studies of Dr. C. G. Jung's contribution to the psychology of the transformation process, at least something of the meaning of this stage seemed to be clarified. In the language of analytic psychology, the transformation is preceded by a strong introversion of the libido, followed by a sort of brooding incubation. Normal sleep itself is manifestly an introversion, and so it is quite understandable that protracted introversion of psychical energy should produce a state of continuous drowsiness. From the standpoint of analytic psychology the introversion of the libido and the incubation are the prior conditions of animation of contents of the unconscious depths of the psyche. I do not think that either von Hartmann or Jung has seen into the nature of the Unconscious as fully as is possible, since their views are limited by the methodology of objective empirical research, aided by intuition, but, judging by the content of their contributions, lack the perspective of direct mystical realization. Nonetheless, I would judge the recorded studies of these two men as lying on the highest level of Western literature. I would rate Dr. Jung, by far, as the greatest Western psychologist, and von Hartmann as a philosopher deserving much higher valuation than he has yet received.

6. At the time of writing *Pathways Through to Space*, one of the purposes was the keeping of a record, not only of the inner processes as far as they lay within the field of consciousness, but as well to note external circumstances that might conceivably have some relevance. I had been acquainted with this as a standard practice of the psychological laboratory where subjects, or human reagents, were required to note bodily and psychical states of themselves, as well as more objective facts, as state of weather, external sounds, etc. This data might or might not have a bearing upon the outcome of a specific experiment, but the fact of its relevance or irrelevance could not be determined until the results of experiment

were later analyzed by the experimenter. I followed this rule of procedure in my record, not necessarily implying that every noted circumstance was significant, but rather aiming to record all that I could think of that might subsequently prove to be significant, although it might seem to have no bearing at the time. One noted circumstance of this sort has proved to be surprisingly significant. At the time of the period of solitude, I was engaged part of the time in the exploration of a gold prospect in the region of the Mother Lode country of California. This entailed considerable periods underground, and while my thought was necessarily engaged a good deal of the time with the concrete details of what I was doing, yet my mind would repeatedly return to reflection upon the material in Shankara's work, which I was reading much of the time when not actually otherwise occupied. At that time I did not know that it was a standard practice in the Orient to place candidates for the transformation inside caves at certain periods, and often for very long periods. It does, indeel, appear that there is some relation between the transformation of "rebirth" and the entering into the earth.

Jung's researches have shown that in the symbolism of the Unconscious, the Unconscious itself is often represented by water and the earth, as well as by other symbols, so that a dream or hypnogogic vision, wherein an individual appears to enter water or the earth, carries the meaning of introversion of the libido into the Unconscious. In connection with the transformation this has the value of entering the womb of the Great Mother Unconscious, preliminary to the Rebirth. Now, there is some mysterious interconnection between the physical ritualistic reproduction of the processes of transformation in dreams and hypnogogic visions and those dreams and visions themselves. That such is the case is at least a tentative conclusion that is forced upon one as one studies the Indian and Tibetan Tantric literature, and the study of western ritualism simply tends to reinforce this conclusion. As I, myself, have never been oriented to ritualism and have never sought from it a personal value, the conclusion forced upon me that it does have important transformation value is quite objective, all the more so as I find in retrospect that I actually performed an exercise, unconscious of what I was doing, which is a conscious practice in the Orient.

That entering the earth, literally, would have a suggestive value to the nonintellectual part of the psyche is at once evident. But I cannot escape the conclusion that more than suggestion is involved. In some manner, actual life springs from the earth and the sea and so there is a sense, more than figurative, that the earth is, indeed, the Mother. Now, anyone who has real acquaintance with the transformation literature from the ancients to our day is bound to be impressed with the widely current rebirth symbolism. Jesus, himself, said, "Ye must be born again." But all life comes from the womb. Nicodemus partly understood Jesus' dictum, but, being a materialist, he could derive only a stupidly literal interpretation. The real gestation of the new Birth is in the womb of the Unconscious, and for this the literal entering of the earth facilitates the process. To find a rationale for this, one must turn to the recurring content of mystical thought. The mystic ever finds the world in complete correspondential relationship with inner psychical realities. Hence, objective relations are not irrelevant, though the degree to which they are determinant varies from individual to individual. With some, slight contact with these objective factors is enough; for others, protracted discipline is necessary.

7. It has come to my mind that the reader might be inclined to question whether this account may be called a narrative description, as I did call it in the last chapter, since so much of the writing is manifestly discursive. However, it really is narrative description, on the whole, since it is a record of a process of thought that took place and had vitally determinant effects in the past. Only in subsidiary degree is this autobiographical material related to the objective life of a physical personality. In much higher degree is it an autobiography of intellectual steps and processes. Thus the discursive material that appears here is primarily not interpretative after fact, but rather part of a process in which interpretative factors were traceably determinant in my own consciousness as it became more and more oriented to the transformation. These interpretations were pragmatically effective agents. Whether or not they have a larger objective truth-value is not the question that is before us at present. Later, I shall return to this larger problem.

8. At the time I was seated out of doors, a fact that may prove to be of some significance. References to a value attained by being under the sky with nothing intervening are to be found in mystical literature. Edward Carpenter has said that he could not write in the vein of *Towards Democracy*

except when he was out of doors under the sky. It is significant that the Sanskrit word Akasha means "sky" as well as "space," "primordial matter," and, in a certain sense, the "higher mind." The sky is the matrix of Light. Thus the sun, the moon, and the stars are embedded in the sky, and the whole sky, from the perspective of the earth, is luminous. Thus, coming from underground out to under the sky is symbolical of leaving the dark place of gestation and entering the Light-world of new birth. That which was hidden becomes revealed; that which was unconscious becomes conscious.

9. The final thought before the 'breakthrough' was the very clear realization that *there was nothing to be attained*. For attainment implied acquisition and acquisition implied change of content in consciousness. But the Goal is not change of content but divorcement from content. Thus Recognition has nothing to do with anything that happens. I am already That which I seek, and therefore, there is nothing to be sought. By the very seeking I hide Myself from myself. Therefore, abandon the search and expect nothing. This was the end of the long search. I died, and in the same instant was born again. Spontaneity took over in place of the old self-determined effort. After that I knew directly the Consciousness possessing the characteristics reported by the mystics again and again. Instead of this process being irrational it is the very apogee of logic. It is reasoned thought carried to the end with mathematical completeness.

10. The Indian and Persian mystics have developed a sensuous poetic imagery for suggesting supernal Value, which reaches far beyond that of the representatives of any western race. To the western mind these portrayals seem extravagant. Actually, however, they are inadequate, since sensuous imagination is crippled at its root by its medium. Mathematical imagination, by being freed from sensuous limitation, soars much higher, but nearly everybody fails to have an appreciation of what has happened. As the reader may be interested in a sample of the Indian imagery, I shall quote a few lines from the opening part of the *Mahanirvana Tantra* (translated by Arthur Avalon):

The enchanting summit of the Lord of Mountains,
resplendent with all its various jewels, clad with many a
tree and many a creeper, melodious with the song of many

a bird, scented with the fragrance of all the season's
flowers, most beautiful, fanned by soft, cool, and perfumed
breezes, shadowed by the still shade of stately trees;
where cool groves resound with the sweet-voiced songs of
troops of Aspara, and in the forest depths flocks of kokila
maddened with passion sing; where (Spring) Lord of the
Seasons with his followers ever abide (the Lord of
Mountains, Kailasa). . . .

The "Lord of the Mountains" is the Door to the Transcendent.

11. The reader is warned that this is still part of the record,
and not the more systematic interpretation after fact. The
contents precipitated into the relative consciousness as a
result of the first insight had a more or less determinant part
in preparing the ground for the culminating Recognition that
came later, and thus are part of the aetiology of the process.

12. By 'superconceptual' I mean beyond the form of all
possible concepts that can be clothed in words. However,
the nature of this knowledge is nearer to that of our purest
concepts than it is to perceptual consciousness.

13. Surely no one will be so clumsy as to suppose this
'universe-sustaining I' is any more the personal 'I' than the
reflection of the sun in water is the real sun itself.

14. The residual personality continues to exist by karma,
and continues to pay prices and reap rewards. But all this
lies below the new base of reference.

15. In my reading some years subsequent to writing this,
I was particularly impressed by a reference to the 'fire' in
C. G. Jung's *Integration of the Personality*. Dr. Jung quotes
an uncanonical saying attributed to the Christ, which runs as
follows: "Whoever is near unto me, is near unto the fire."
(p. 141) Here, also, identification with the 'fire' is implied,
as well as effects upon those who are near. Fire is that which
burns up and so transforms (sublimates) everything except
the ash. To understand these mystical uses of words one must
isolate and idealize the essential functions of the corresponding
literal or physical process.

16. At the time of the transformation I called this joy-
filled 'force' the "Current." The latter term broke into my

mind spontaneously and was not the result of an objective reflective search for a descriptive term. A 'sense of flow' is an immediate fact of the state, to be distinguished from the objective interpretative judgment: 'It is a flow'. The step from the immediately given to the conceptual interpretation involves the problem of criticism, which I shall have to face later. But this much I may say here—there are interpretations that one feels at once are substantially true to the sense of the immediate value, while others falsify it. True, in this spirit, was the description I gave of the seeming of the Flow. I said it was a Flow that did not proceed from the past to the future, but rather, turned upon itself so that there was continuous motion with no progress or decline. I later found that this conception evoked no intelligible meaning in minds that were mystically blind. Certainly, in the sense of objective reference, it is meaningless; nonetheless I must still affirm its substantial truth with respect to the sense of the immediate realization. At the time I was not familiar with analogous references in mystical literature, but I have found them since. Thus, in the *Secret of the Golden Flower* the "circulation of the Light" stands as the critical accomplishment of the 'Great Work.' In this, among other effects, immortality is accomplished. Now, analysis of the symbol helps a good deal. Thus the "circulation" suggests self-containedness, while the straight line of chronological time has direction and is therefore dogged by the pairs of opposites. The time-line does not progress any more than it degrades. It gives life and takes it away. Hence, the philosophic pessimist is the one who has seen deeply. Only through the "circulation of the Light" is the tragedy of world-life mastered.

17. The first time I experienced the consciousness of benevolence certain consequences were striking. At the time, I was sitting in a very humble shack, quite alone, located on one of the creeks of the Mother Lode country of east central California. Insects and other creatures were rather overfamiliar companions. Spiders, scorpions, daddy longlegs (in great numbers), centipedes, slugs, gnats, and rattlesnakes were creatures one could never safely forget. But when the state of benevolence was superimposed upon my own private consciousness, it included all these creatures as much as any other. My goodwill included them equally with more evolved beings, and there was nothing forced in the attitude. It was no conscious moral victory, but just a state of natural feeling.

This state of immediate feeling is transient just as is true of other phases of mystical states of consciousness. But it leaves a permanent effect upon the moral judgment. One can no longer kill anything, no matter how repulsive or destructive it may seem, without a feeling of guilt. This definitely increases the difficulty of objective life. For when the individual sees the objective realities clearly, he finds that there is no embodied living in this world that does not imply killing, and, therefore, guilt. The farmer must destroy the enemies of his plants and stock, or have the latter destroyed, and without the farmer no man has food. And then, within our blood there is constant war, with tiny creatures being killed and devoured all the time. Hence, all life here depends upon the taking of life. It is a very ugly world that comes into view when the blinders are removed from the eyes. Saints (who continue to live) and vegetarians share the guilt with all the rest. The amount of guilt does vary, of course, but difference of degree is not a difference of principle. All men who live in this world inevitably share guilt, and thus there are none who may cast the first stone. There are none who may sit in judgment upon others, unless at the same time they judge themselves and accept sentence along with the others. Release from guilt lies only in the Beyond.

18. There is at times a spontaneous upwelling that leads to the most effective production, but at the same time there is conscious selection and judging upon the part of the mind that was trained in the schools. The resultant product is thus a joint product of deeper and more superficial levels, both part of myself. I might suggest this compound action by a figure. If we were to think of the mental accumulations of a lifetime as being filed away in a sort of hall of records in which there is only a dim illumination so that, ordinarily, much of the material is hard to locate, and therefore not easily used, the state of illumination is like a brilliant light suddenly appearing in that hall that renders everything filed, at once available. The light has the additional effect of leading well nigh unerringly to the most appropriate selection of the material that is pertinent to the problem in hand. The once known and forgotten tends to become known again, and all this without laborious trying.

19. Thus, according to the handed-down record, Gautama Buddha discouraged the practicing of the trance state, though

He did not repudiate it as a possible means. Yet, Samadhi is a fundamental part of the Buddhist Way. The implication is that bodily condition is essentially irrelevant.

20. A study of the word "ecstasy" in an adequate dictionary clarifies a good deal that is confusing about the word as it is employed in literature, particularly that of a medical sort. As the term is of high importance in relation to mysticism, this study is very helpful. The dictionary gives four uses, which cover a wide range of meanings, and I shall quote these in full. Ecstasy is defined (see *Century Dictionary and Cyclopedia*) as:

a. "A state in which the mind is exalted or liberated, as it were, from the body; a state in which the functions of the senses are suspended by the contemplation of some extraordinary or supernatural object, or by absorption in some overpowering idea, most frequently of a religious nature; entrancing rapture or transport.

b. "Overpowering emotion or exaltation, in which the mind is absorbed and the actions are controlled by the exciting subject; a sudden access of intense feeling.

c. "In medicine, a morbid state of the nervous system, allied to catalepsy or trance, in which the patient assumes the attitude and expression of rapture. ('Ecstasis' is a synonym for this usage.)

d. "Insanity; madness."

Etymologically, the word carries the meaning of "any displacement or removal from the proper place, a standing aside."

From the external point of view all four meanings are consistent with the etymological sense of the word. But in the intensive sense the difference of meaning is as great as the difference between a snake and an eel, which are only analogous but not homologous. In the sense of the first meaning the "displacement from the proper place" is true only on the assumption that personal egoism is the proper place. It is a prime thesis of mystical philosophy that this assumption is a fundamental error.

The primary meaning of the Sanscrit word "Samadhi" reveals a much more profound insight into the real meaning of mystical Ecstasy. "Samadhi" has the significance of "putting together, joining with; union; combination; performance; adjustment, settlement; justification of a statement; proof; attention, intentness on; deep meditation on the supreme soul, profound devotion." Thus the prime meaning is that of "bringing together of that which is improperly separated". This gives a value that is highly positive and superior, while the etymology of 'ecstasy' is depreciatory. It is a difference of viewpoint that parallels that between the Ptolemaic and the Copernican systems, with the profounder Indian view corresponding to placing the center in the sun. The typically ancient Greek orientation was not spiritual but sensuous-materialistic, the philosophers of the type of Plato and Plotinus being the exceptions. The Greeks realized bodies rather than space. Hence a consciousness which stood disassociated from bodies appeared as not in the proper place. The general Greek insight is not as profound as supposed. It is the great exceptions who have lived to our day, just because they have seen more truly, and while these have deserved the honor we have given them, they have not justified us in extending that honor to the Greek civilization as a whole. Our own spatially oriented mathematics is nearer to the feeling of the Indian than the typical Greek.

21. So long as there is contrast and not indifference to the contrasting elements, the state is not nirdvandva—freed from the pairs of opposites. The feeling of superlative value is, after all, a dualistic state. In a genuinely absolute state there is not, and could not be, any preference whatsoever. A consciousness of Bliss, of All Knowledge, or of Compassion is thus colored with something relative, so long as it is felt or known that there is anything else with different value. Any possible report of the state of nirdvandva inevitably seems to the relative consciousness as nothing at all. This adequately explains why the unillumined psychologists view the highest of mystical states of consciousness as identical with unconsciousness. There is a serious error in this interpretation, but only he who has known the actuality immediately can know, and he cannot tell what he knows to one who does not also know. One can only categorically affirm: "It is not unconscious." However, it is as little like what is ordinarily understood to be consciousness as to be indistinguishable from unconsciousness as viewed from the relative perspective.

22. The manuals are generally, if not universally, insistent upon mental quiescence and emotional calmness. I am not here developing a critique of the manuals but simply reporting what actually happened. But there may be a valid need of such a critique.

23. The reader must have patience with these unusual combinations of conceptions if he would acquire any understanding at all. There is no word-combination that is strictly true to the meaning intended, and so the common medium is strained to suggest a most uncommon content. In any case, there is mystery enough in the relation of idea to its referent, even in ordinary usage. Habit has caused most of us to neglect this mystery, but it has led to the production of many volumes out of the minds of philosophers.

24. When to wish for is to have immediately, it is impossible to isolate desire from possession. The awareness of desire necessarily vanishes. Ordinarily we desire and achieve the object only imperfectly after much effort. Thus we are highly conscious of desire. If there were absolutely no barrier to *complete* fulfillment, there could be no more consciousness of desiring.

25. This is clearly a case of dialectic flow paralleling the thesis, antithesis, and synthesis of Hegelian logic. Corresponding to the thesis is consciousness conditioned by desire, to the antithesis is the State of Satisfaction, and to the synthesis the State of High Indifference. Hegel is correct in viewing the process as autonomous. However, I think we can trace the vital logic a little more in detail. There could be no satisfaction without an antecedent felt lack, from which desire grows. But at the moment lack vanishes, satisfaction withers as does a tree of which the roots are cut. Then the dualism is dissolved, leaving a nondual state, which, affectively and conatively considered, is Indifference.

26. At this point I must take radical exception to the thesis of Dr. Jung given in the first chapter of *The Integration of the Personality*. There Jung says: "In the end, consciousness becomes vast but dim . . ." It is no more dim than acute. It is really nirdvandva, and no contrasting description is really valid.

27. Surely, no one would be so stupid as to imagine that this is a personal power. The great power of the sun is not wholly manifested in the image of the sun reflected in the drop of water. Inwardly, *I* am the Sun, but as a personal ego I am the *image* of the Sun lying in the drop.

28. It was sometime after writing this that I became

acquainted with the one figure in western history who reveals something of the great Buddha's depth of penetration. I refer to Meister Eckhart, recognized by some as the greatest mystic of the middle ages, and in my judgment one of the greatest in western history. He is the only instance I have found in the West, so far, who reveals acquaintance with what I have called the High Indifference. In other words than mine he has expressed the same meaning as that given above, thus: "For man is truly God, and God truly man." Also, in the same spirit some centuries later the poet Angelus Silesius (Johann Scheffler) wrote in beautiful simplicity:

> I am as great as God,
> And He is small like me;
> He cannot be above,
> Nor I below Him be.

There are always to be found witnesses of the Eternal Truth. (Quotations taken from Jung's *Psychological Types*.)

29. See James's use of the terms 'thick' and 'thin' in the *Pluralistic Universe*.

30. We are throughout all this presentation confronted with the old philosophic problem of Illusion and Reality. It is involved in all the great monistic philosophies. It appears that William James, at one stage in his philosophic life, earnestly strived to resolve certain fundamental difficulties inherent in such philosophies, at least in their western form. His effort failed and he gave up monism entirely, advancing in its place a frankly pluralistic philosophy. While he did not dogmatically close the door to the possibility of a speculative resolution of the problem, he left the impression of grave doubt that such resolution existed. James saw quite clearly that there are different states of consciousness that are ineluctable facts. If these are represented by the twenty-six letters of the alphabet, then the unity of them all would not be simply one fact, but the twenty-seventh fact. Thus there is no resolution of many-ness into unity.

James's critical analysis is acute and is probably sound if we restrict ourselves to the limitations of Aristotelian logic. But this is not the whole of logic, as is evidenced by the development of the logic of relatives, not to mention the dialectic of Hegel. There is no good reason to suppose that current western knowledge of logic is the whole of logic. Now, there is a logical principle that, I believe, so far clarifies the problem as to render the speculative resolution much more probable. I shall introduce the principle by reference to a very common oriental figure.

People who live in a country where venemous serpents are a serious hazard are familiar with the delusion of seeing a snake that is not there. We who have been much in the wilds of the far West know this delusion quite well. One early learns to be everlastingly on guard, so that near the surface of his mind he is always watching for snakes. Often it happens that a stick, piece of rope, or other long slim object will be perceived, half unconsciously, and lead to a reaction of the organism before rational recognition of the object is possible. One seems to see a snake, feels the shock, pauses, and perhaps jumps, before a rational judgment is possible. A moment later he sees his error. I have had this experience many times, and on analysis find that it reveals a great deal. The snake, at first seemingly seen, a moment later is a stick, rope, or such other material object as it may be. The question then is, What happened to the snake? Did a snake become a stick? a rope? The final practical judgment is that the snake did not become a stick, but never was there. Yet there is no doubt that, in a psychical sense, experience of snake was there. Well, then, what is the nature of its existence? We certainly do not attribute to it substantial reality. It assuredly cannot bite or otherwise be dangerous in an objective sense. The moment after the rational recognition and judgment, there simply is no snake. Further—and this subtle point is the very crux of the matter—*the snake ceases to have ever been*. I know that the process works this way since I have observed it again and again. It remains true that there had been a state of psychical delusion, yet there is a vitally important sense in which the snake ceases to be, both as a present and past fact. The delusion neither added anything to the reality nor took anything away. There is thus no problem as to how to integrate it within reality.

Now, the speculative resolution of the monist's problem is found by applying the above principle of interpretation to the whole of relative experience. The latter differs from the snake experience in that it is massively collective and is, generally, not at once corrected by a rational recognition and judgment. It is to be viewed as like unto a vast delusional insanity and is to be corrected as a dream-problem is corrected, simply by waking up. Human suffering is of like nature to the suffering of the delusionally insane, and there is no real cure in terms of the premise of the insane state.

But what is the difference between reality and delusion, since the delusion is a psychical fact? Simply this. The reality is substantial, while the delusion is empty. In Buddhist terms, the only actuality in the delusional modification of consciousness lies in its being of one sameness with the essence of mind, but there is no actuality of content. All experience is simply the revelry of mind and has no substance in itself.

The adequacy of the snake-rope analogy has been ably challenged by Sri Aurobindo Ghose in his *The Life Divine*, with the consequent introduction of doubt as to the objective validity of the figure. However, the analogy does seem to be subjectively valid since the relative consciousness tends to vanish, like the snake into the rope, while the self-consciousness is immersed in the Transcendent. It appears that Aurobindo has made necessary a reexamination of the classical metaphysical theories grounded upon realizations of the above sort. This subject will be considered later in the present work.

31. The main text of this chapter was written and completed toward the end of March 1937, just after finishing the text *Pathways Through to Space*. The footnotes were added seven years later. The latter reflect the expanded perspective afforded by a quite considerable study of the transformation problem, both in western psychological sources and in Buddhist sources that had not been available for me prior to the cycle reported. Though the problem has not had a wide consideration, it has attracted the attention of some of the best minds the world has ever known. I know now that although the ground covered has only rarely been traversed as far, to judge by the mystical records, yet all the Way has been pioneered long ago. This simply reveals the fundamental universality of the problem.

PART II

The Aphorisms on Consciousness Without an Object

Chapter 3

THE
LEVELS OF
THOUGHT

●

In the semiesoteric psychology of Buddhism, Vedantism, and Theosophy, there is to be found a division of
Mind into two parts or facets.[1] While it is affirmed
that the essence of mind is unitary, yet in the process
of manifestation mind becomes like a two-faced mirror,
one face oriented to the objective, the other to the
subjective. Since the mind functions in considerable
measure like a mirror, it takes on the appearance of
that which it reflects, and thus its own essential nature
tends to become hidden. The objectively oriented facet
reflects the world and is colored by the conative-affec-

tive nature of the personal man. The inwardly directed facet, like that which it reflects, is marked by the undistorting colorlessness of dispassion.[2] But since both facets are of one and the same essence, there is a native affinity between them. Because of this, the consciousness of man, by the appropriate means, is enabled to cross what would otherwise be an impassible gulf of unconsciousness. This is not to say that the empiric or personal man, if unpossessed of mind, would actually have no connection with his roots, but it would mean that the relation is unconscious in the strict sense. Through the doubly reflecting mind of one essence it becomes possible, in principle, for the personally integrated consciousness to know the roots. Thus there is a Way whereby man may know the transcendent.

For western psychology and much of western philosophy the acquaintance with mind is restricted to the outwardly oriented facet of the oriental conception. This is true for the reason that the exclusively objective methods of occidental science, at the outset, exclude the possibility of direct acquaintance with the more hidden facet. There would be little or no harm in this if it were realized that only a facet, and not the whole, was the real object of study, but all too commonly it is inferred that the method employed can provide conclusions justifying privative judgments. Thus we have the widely held attitude that the total possibilities of human consciousness are exclusively of the type that are true enough of the objective facet of mind. This standpoint simply is unsound, and this unsoundness can be verified by the appropriate means. Here science, in the familiar western sense, does not mean "to know fully," but rather "to know restrictedly," and therefore does not justify privative judgments. SCIENCE, in the sense of knowing fully, cannot be restricted to objective material, but must, as well, be open to other possibilities of awareness. Western psychology is limited in its possibilities through a restriction imposed at its roots by methodological presuppositions. Accordingly, mind can never be known in its totality by this means.

As it appears through the western method of research, the mind tends to appear as quite lacking in self-determination. Thinking seems to be entrained behind wishing and unable long to continue on its own momentum. Thus the conception has grown that thinking is only instrumental to action, the latter being the direct outgrowth of the conative factor in consciousness. Clearly, such a view greatly restricts the supposedly valid zone of the judgments of thought. Among other consequences it excludes the possibility of a genuine knowledge of the transcendent, which is just the center of focus in the present work.

It is a tribute to the relative competency of western psychologic methodology that the derived interpretation of mind functioning is in substantial agreement with the oriental psychology with respect to the lower facet. This latter is often designated kama manas, but since kama is the Sanscrit equivalent of 'desire', we derive the meaning of 'desire mind', and this is very easily identified with thinking led by wishfulness. Wishfulness in thinking is undoubtedly a *part* truth, but it is not the whole truth.

No one may validly affirm the truth of a read or spoken statement merely because he has read it or heard it. Western science is by no means more insistent upon this than was the great Buddha himself. Indeed, the latter was the more exacting of the two. The individual must verify for himself, or at least be able to do so, before he may justifiably accept, save as possibility. Thus we cannot affirm the actuality of the inner facet of mind until we know it directly, as no more is ignorance competent to deny its actuality. I affirm the actuality of the inner facet on the ground of direct acquaintance, and further affirm that it may be known directly, through the transformation process, by any one who fulfills the conditions.

There is another kind of thought, dispassionate and self-directing, that stands in contrast with the thought that is guided by wishing. It may be said that this thought thinks itself, or tends to do so, depending upon the degree of its purity. It is not concerned with the preconceptions of the relative consciousness nor with the pragmatic interest of man. It tends to be authoritarian in its form, and while possessed of its own logic, yet ignores or tends to ignore that part of logical process oriented to objective referents. Most readily it expresses itself in aphoristic form, with more or less dissociation of statement from statement. But this dissociation is a surface appearance only. An analogous form is to be noted in the groups of postulates that form the bases of formally developed systems of mathematics that by themselves do not give an explicit logical whole, but rather provide the components from which a logical whole may be developed. However, the genuine aphorism differs from most groups of mathematical postulates in that the latter are generally inventions of the unillumined mind, while the aphorism is a spontaneous production out of an illumined state. They could well serve as postulates from which systematic logical development could be constructed, in which case they might well be conceived as authentic *axioms* and not merely as *fundamental assumptions*. Something of the character of this thought I have been able to isolate, and thus have been enabled to see somewhat of the root whence springs the aphoristic thought.

There are certainly four kinds of thought that I find discernible, with various gradations and intermixtures. Of these, three employ or can employ verbal concepts with more or less adequacy. The fourth has no relation whatsoever with any possible word-concept, as far as its inner content is concerned. Thus the latter is not related to communication as between different centers of consciousness. The other three serve communication in some sense.

In its most lowly form, thought is inextricably entangled with bodily existence. Here thought serves organic need and relation. It is the commonest thought of everybody and is not wholly beyond the comprehension of animals. This is the thought in absolute bondage to desire, which has no value save as it serves organism. Obviously it has no eternal worth. Its language may be just as well the grunt or the gesture as the more highly developed word.

Above this is a thought well known to cultured man. It is the thought of the liberated or partly liberated concept, and is thus the thought for which the word is the peculiarly adapted vehicle. This is the thought out of which grow science, philosophy, mathematics, and much of art. It is extremely articulate. In some manifestations it attains a high order of purity, but may be more or less contaminated with the inferior kind of thought. Most actual human thinking is such a contamination. Even those who have known this thought on its levels of greater purity cannot maintain themselves at the requisite pitch of discipline during a large proportion of waking consciousness. It is consciously directed thinking and is achieved at the price of fatiguing labor. The writing here, at this moment, is of this class.

At the deepest level of discernible thought there is

a thinking that flows of itself. In its purity it employs none of the concepts that could be captured in definable words. It is fluidic rather than granular. It never isolates a definitive divided part but everlastingly interblends with all. Every thought includes the whole of Eternity, and yet there are distinguishable thoughts. The unbroken Eternal flows before the mind, yet is endlessly colored anew with unlimited possibility. There is no labor in this thought. It simply is. It is unrelated to all desiring, all images, and all symbols.

Between the deepest level of thought and the conscious and laborious thought, there is a fourth kind that, in a sense, is the child of these two. In high degree, this thought flows of itself, yet blends with verbal concepts. Here the conceptual thought and the transcendent thought combine in mutual action. But the lowly thought of the organic being has no part in this. It is a thought that is sweet and true, but fully clear only to him who has Vision.

The best of poetry has much of this kind of thought. It is the poetry that stirs the souls rather than the senses of men. It is the poetry of content rather than of form. But most of all, from this level of thought are born the aphorisms, that strange kind of thought that is both poetry and something more. For it stirs the thinking as well as the feeling and thus integrates the best of the whole man. Mystery is an inextricable part of this thought.

It should not be hard to recognize in the transcendental thought and the organic thought the purest forms of the superior and inferior facets of mind. The conceptual and aphoristic thinking are derivatives from these.

It is a misconception that conceptual thought is

exclusively a child of the organic kind of thinking—
something that developed *solely* to serve the adaptation
of a living organism to its environment as the difficulties became more complex. It has possibilities of detachment that could never have been born out of
organic life. At its best, it is more than lightly colored
with the dispassionate otherworldliness of the transcendental thought. Something of both the transcendental and the organic is in it, sometimes more of one,
at other times more of the other.

It is in the realm of this kind of thought that the
West has outdistanced the East. It is peculiarly a
western power. Its potential office in the transformation process is not to be found in the oriental manuals.
Here we face new possibilities.

The aphoristic thought is the child of the transcendental and the conceptual. This is the highest form of
articulate thought. He who would understand cannot
do so with his conceptual powers alone. He must also
let the understanding grow up from within him.

Notes to Chapter 3

1. In this instance I am using 'mind' as a synonym of
'manas'. While this practice is quite common, it is far from
being strictly correct. The western definition and usage of
"mind" is a good deal wider than that of 'manas', which has
a specifically restricted meaning. For fuller discussion of this
see *Pathways Through to Space*, p. 193.

2. The distinction between the two facets of the mind
seems to be approximately, if not identically, that given by
Sri Aurobindo in his *The Life Divine* in his usage of the
conceptions of "surface mind" and "subliminal mind."

Chapter 4

APHORISMS ON CON- SCIOUSNESS WITHOUT AN OBJECT

●

1 . . . Consciousness-without-an-object is.

●

2 . . . Before objects were,
Consciousness-without-an-object is.

(((101)))

•

3 . . . Though objects seem to exist,
Consciousness-without-an-object is.

•

4 . . . When objects vanish,
yet remaining through all unaffected,
Consciousness-without-an-object is.

•

5 . . . Outside of Consciousness-without-an-object
nothing is.

•

6 ... Within the bosom of
Consciousness-without-an-object lies
the power of awareness that projects objects.

●

7 ... When objects are projected,
the power of awareness as subject is presupposed,
yet Consciousness-without-an-object
remains unchanged.

●

8 ... When consciousness of objects is born, then,
likewise, consciousness of absence of objects arises.

●

9 ... Consciousness of objects is the Universe.

●

10 . . . Consciousness of absence of objects
is Nirvana.

●

11 . . . Within Consciousness-without-an-object
lie both the Universe and Nirvana,
yet to Consciousness-without-an-object
these two are the same.

●

12 . . . Within Consciousness-without-an-object
lies the seed of Time.

●

13 . . . When awareness cognizes Time then
knowledge of Timelessness is born.

●

14 . . . To be aware of Time is to be aware of
the Universe, and to be aware of the Universe
is to be aware of Time.

●

15 . . . To realize Timelessness is to attain Nirvana.

●

16 . . . But for Consciousness-without-an-object
there is no difference between
Time and Timelessness.

●

17 . . . Within Consciousness-without-an-object
lies the seed of the world-containing Space.

●

18 . . . When awareness cognizes the
world-containing Space then knowledge of
the Spatial Void is born.

●

19 . . . To be aware of the world-containing Space
is to be aware of the Universe of Objects.

●

20 . . . To realize the Spatial Void
is to awaken to Nirvanic Consciousness.

•

21 . . . But for Consciousness-without-an-object
there is no difference between the world-containing
Space and the Spatial Void.

•

22 . . . Within Consciousness-without-an-object
lies the Seed of Law.

•

23 . . . When consciousness of objects is born
the Law is invoked as a Force
tending ever toward Equilibrium.

•

24 . . . All objects exist as tensions within Consciousness-without-an-object that tend ever to flow into their own complements or others.

•

25 . . . The ultimate effect of the flow of all objects into their complements is mutual cancellation in complete Equilibrium.

•

26 . . . Consciousness of the field of tensions is the Universe.

•

27 . . . Consciousness of Equilibrium is Nirvana.

●

28 . . . But for Consciousness-without-an-object there is neither tension nor Equilibrium.

●

29 . . . The state of tensions is the state of ever-becoming.

●

30 . . . Ever-becoming is endless-dying.

●

31 . . . So the state of consciousness of objects
is a state of ever-renewing promises
that pass into death at the moment of fulfillment.

●

32 . . . Thus when consciousness is attached to
objects the agony of birth and death never ceases.

●

33 . . . In the state of Equilibrium
where birth cancels death
the deathless Bliss of Nirvana is realized.

●

34 . . . But Consciousness-without-an object
is neither agony nor bliss.

●

35 . . . Out of the Great Void,
which is Consciousness-without-an-object,
the Universe is creatively projected.

●

36 . . . The Universe as experienced is the
created negation that ever resists.

●

37 . . . The creative act is bliss,
the resistance, unending pain.

●

38 . . . *Endless resistance is the*
Universe of experience; the agony of crucifixion.

●

39 . . . *Ceaseless creativeness is Nirvana,*
the Bliss beyond human conceiving.

●

40 . . . *But for Consciousness-without-an-object*
there is neither creativeness nor resistance.

●

*41 . . . Ever-becoming and ever-ceasing-to-be
are endless action.*

●

*42 . . . When ever-becoming cancels the
ever-ceasing-to-be then Rest is realized.*

●

43 . . . Ceaseless action is the Universe.

●

44 . . . Unending Rest is Nirvana.

●

45 . . . But Consciousness-without-an-object
is neither Action nor Rest.

●

46 . . . When consciousness is attached to objects
it is restricted through the forms imposed by
the world-containing Space, by Time, and by Law.

●

47 . . . When consciousness is disengaged from
objects, Liberation from the forms of the
world-containing Space, of Time, and of Law
is attained.

●

48 . . . Attachment to objects is
consciousness bound within the Universe.

●

49 . . . Liberation from such attachment is
the State of unlimited Nirvanic Freedom.

●

50 . . . But Consciousness-without-an-object
is neither bondage nor freedom.

●

51 . . . Consciousness-without-an-object
may be symbolized by a SPACE that is
unaffected by the presence or absence of objects,
for which there is neither Time nor Timelessness;
neither a world-containing Space nor a Spatial Void,
neither Tension nor Equilibrium;
neither Resistance nor Creativeness;
neither Agony nor Bliss; neither Action nor Rest;
and neither Restriction nor Freedom.

•

52 . . . As the GREAT SPACE is not to be
identified with the Universe,
so neither is It to be identified with any Self.

•

53 . . . The GREAT SPACE is not God,
but the comprehender of all Gods,
as well as of all lesser creatures.

•

54 . . . The GREAT SPACE, or
Consciousness-without-an-object, is the
Sole Reality upon which all objects
and all selves depend and derive their existence.

•

55 . . . The GREAT SPACE comprehends both the
Path of the Universe and the Path of Nirvana.

●

56 . . . Beside the GREAT SPACE
there is none other.

●

OM TAT SAT

●

Chapter 5

GENERAL DISCUSSION OF CON- SCIOUSNESS WITHOUT AN OBJECT

●

The aphorisms that constitute the material of the preceding chapter are to be regarded as a symbolic representation of the culminating stage of the Recognition reported in the second chapter of Part I. The direct value of that Recognition is inexpressible and inconceivable in the sense of concepts meaning just what they are defined to mean and no more. Of necessity, all concepts deal with content in some sense, as they are born in the tension of a subject aware of objects and refer to objects. Consciousness-without-an-object is not an object on the level where it is realized. But just as soon as words are employed to refer to it, we have in place of the actuality a sort of shadowy reflection. This reflection may be useful as a symbol pointing toward the Reality, but becomes a deception just as soon as it is regarded as a comprehensive concept. Conceivable conclusions may be derived from the original symbol, but the full realization of That which is symbolized requires the dissolving of the very power of representation itself.

There are two lines of approach to, and employment of, the aphorisms. They may be regarded as seeds to be taken into the meditative state, in which case they will tend to arouse the essentially inexpressible Meaning and Realization which they symbolize. This we may call their mystical value. On the other hand, they may be regarded as primary indefinables upon which a systematic philosophy of the universe and its negation, Nirvana, may be developed. In this case, they may be viewed as a base of reference from which all thought and experience may be evaluated. From the standpoint of strict logic, they would have to be regarded as arbitrary in the same sense as the fundamental assumptions of any system of mathematics are logically arbitrary. For any individual to determine whether they are more than arbitrary would require a direct Gnostic Realization of the Truth symbolized by them, but for the individual lacking such a Realization, they may be evaluated as any system of pure mathematics or work of art is commonly evaluated. In the latter case they are justified if they enrich the consciousness of man, entirely apart from any determination of their ontological validity. I offer the aphorisms to the reader in this sense, if he is unable to find any more fundamental justification for them.

It is a fundamental principle of this philosophy that the aphorisms are not derived from experience. In its employment here I have restricted the term "experience" to the meaning formulated in Baldwin's *Dictionary of Philosophy and Psychology*. This rules out definitely any state of consciousness that may have an absolute or timeless character as being properly regarded as experience. It is a primary consideration that experience should be defined as a time-conditioned state of consciousness in which events or processes transpire. Whether or not thought with its products may be regarded as a part of experience, and likewise whether "experience" is to be restricted to the "raw immediacy" of phenomena before it is analysed by reflective thought is unimportant for my present purposes. It is important, simply, that "experience" should be understood as time conditioned. This seems to be sufficiently consonant with the meaning of the term as it is employed in the various empiric philosophies. So, when it is predicated that the aphorisms are not derived from experience, it is meant that they are derivative from a consciousness that is not conditioned by time. Of course, their formulation was an event and a process in time, but it is only as symbols that they are time conditioned. Their meaning and authority inhere in that which is beyond experience.

I am well aware that several philosophies affirm or imply that all consciousness is of necessity time conditioned. But since this is undemonstrable, it has only the value of arbitrary assertion, which is countered by simple denial. This affirmation or implication is incompatible with the basis realized or assumed here— whichever way it may be taken. At this point I simply deny the validity of the affirmation and assert that there is a Root Consciousness that is not time conditioned. It may be valid enough to assert that human consciousness qua human is always time conditioned, but that would amount merely to a partial definition of what is meant by human consciousness. In that case, the consciousness that is not time conditioned would be something that is transhuman or nonhuman. I am entirely willing to accept this view, but would add that it is in the power of man to transcend the limits of human consciousness and thus come to a more or less complete understanding of the factors that limit the range of human consciousness qua human. The term "human" would thus define a certain range in the scale of consciousness—something like an octave in the scale of electromagnetic waves. In that case, the present system implies that it is, in principle, possible for a conscious being to shift his field of consciousness up and down the scale. When such an entity is focused within the human octave it might be agreed to call him human, but something other than human when focused in other octaves. Logically, this is simply a matter of definition of terms, and I am more than willing to regard the human as merely a stage in consciousness, provided it is not asserted dogmatically that it is impossible for consciousness and self-identity to flow from stage to stage. On the basis of such a definition this philosophy would not be a contribution to Humanism but to Transhumanism.

The Critique of Pure Reason I regard as a philosophical work of very high importance. The most significant conclusion of that work seems to be that the pure reason, acting by itself, cannot solve the ontological problems. The reason can work upon a material that is given, but cannot, itself, supply the original material. If material is given through experience, then the reason can derive consequences that are also valid within the field of experience. However, the reason operates within the matrix of a transcendental base, and thus is something more than experience, though it be ever so impossible to recognize and isolate reason before the conscious being has had experience. The transcendental base is a preexistence determined after the fact of experience. Now, if we regard Kant's criticism as a sort of circumscription of a certain field of consciousness, his work may well be permanently valid in its main outlines. I am disposed to think that it is. But I question whether his analysis was broad enough to cover the whole field of human consciousness. It would seem to fit more especially that particular phase of human consciousness in which lies western scientific knowledge. In any case, it is not an analysis of sub-human consciousness, such as that of the animal, nor is it competent as a study of the forms of consciousness realized in the various mystical states.

For my own part, I do not contend that the pure reason, either acting in a strictly formal sense or upon a material given by experience, can demonstrate a transcendental reality. On the contrary, this reality must be realized immediately, if it is to have more than a hypothetical existence. But assuming that a given individual has awakened to a transcendental realization, it is possible for him to reflect the transcendent through concepts, when the latter are taken in a symbolic sense. Such concepts may then serve as original material upon which the reason can operate and derive consequences. Some or all of these consequences may well prove to have value within the range of relative consciousness, including experience. I do not suggest that such a system will necessarily prove competent to render experience, as such, unnecessary. It may only supply that which experience, by itself, cannot supply, i.e., an integrative framework capable of comprehending all possible experience however unpredictable its specific quale may be. Experience as raw immediacy does not define its own meaning. A given "raw immediacy" cast in the framework of traditional Christian theology arouses a meaning that is quite different from that afforded when the base of reference is such as is assumed by physical science. Neither of these frameworks are derived from nor proved by experience. Logically, they are simply presuppositions from which observation, analysis, and interpretation proceed. Historically, each has supplied human consciousness with positive values, and for that reason has persisted over considerable periods of time. But today we know that both are inadequate. Our science has given command over external nature that the older theology failed to achieve, but in turn it leaves a very important part of the demands of human consciousness unsatisfied—a fact that is exemplified by the growth of psychosis and parapsychosis.

A transcendental reality cannot be proved by logic nor can it be experienced in the time-bound sense, but it may be *realized* mystically. It is impossible to prove the actuality of God, freedom, immortality, or any other supposed metaphysical reality, in the scientific sense of proof. With respect to these matters, either to affirm or to deny is unscientific. The competency of any scientist qua scientist need not be affected by either an attitude of belief or of disbelief. But an attitude of belief or disbelief may make a lot of difference to him as a complete human being. There is an enormous divergence between a human consciousness that is rich and filled with assurance compared to one that is starved and uncertain, and this difference is important to relative life itself, even though not affecting technical scientific competency. Practically, men assume much that they do not know and that cannot be known within the limits of the methodology of physical science. In spite of themselves, men do act upon transcendental assumptions, even when the assumption is in the form of a denial of the possibility of a transcendental reality. And all this does make a difference for life as actually lived.

The man who has not realized the transcendental, in the mystical sense of realization, is not freed from the necessity of acting "as if" with respect to some transcendental base that forms his outlook on life. Barring mystic certainty, the relative merits of one "as if" when compared to others is to be judged by the values afforded for life as actually lived. No dogmatist, whether ecclesiastical or scientific, has any right to challenge the freedom of any man in the selection of his purely transcendental "as if." Such an "as if" can never contradict the raw immediacy of experience, since the former is related to value or meaning, which is another dimension of consciousness entirely. For instance, a scientific determination that the secretions of the ductless glands, in the case of a given individual, differ from the norm, proves nothing concerning the value of the consciousness enjoyed by the individual. The deviation from the norm may or may not be favorable for a long life, but in any case this is irrelevant when we measure the value of the consciousness in question. We are simply dealing with another dimension of consciousness altogether.

The aphorisms may be regarded as affording a particular "as if" basis for integrating in terms of value the totality of relative consciousness. In this case, it is unnecessary to raise the question as to whether they are true or false in the scientific sense. In fact, they are neither true nor false when these judgments are employed as they are in physical science. They stand simply as the basis for the integration of relative consciousness. They may be viewed as of only psychological significance, though for me there is no doubt concerning their positive metaphysical rooting. They are not a mere "as if" for me, though I am quite willing to assume the "as if" status for them as a minimal basis for the purpose of discourse. However, entirely apart from the question of metaphysical actuality, it remains true that there is an enormous practical difference between a self that is out of harmony with the not-self and a self that has attained harmonious integration with the not-self. The steps toward such harmonious integration in their less comprehensive phases are known as "conversion," and when more profoundly developed, as "mystical awakening." That these aphorisms have the power to produce such transformations I have already demonstrated empirically in connection with others than myself. This fact, alone, is sufficient to vindicate their use as an "as if" basis, at least in principle.

In his *Dance of Life*, Havelock Ellis has developed the thesis that both science and philosophy are arts and therefore have the same justification as any other art, at the very least. This is to say that both are creative constructions, whatever else they may be. In this respect Havelock Ellis's position is consonant with my own. It simply means that a real philosophy is a Way of Life, however much it may also be a system of notions. I regard the aphorisms as affording a base that is valid in both senses. However, criticism may give them quite different evaluation, depending upon the sense taken. In any case, I insist upon their value in determining a Way of Life. That is to say, that before and above all other ways, they determine a religious attitude. But for me, individually, no religious attitude is satisfactory that is not, at least, philosophically and mathematically adequate, and ultimately, justly comprehensive of all phases of consciousness. However, I ask the reader to view, and if possible, to accept this philosophy as he would a work of art, even though he can go no farther.

The basis of integration afforded by the aphorisms is that of the radical assertion of the primacy of Consciousness. In this respect the present thesis stands in a position counter to that of the so-called scientific philosophies. In the case of the latter, matter, things, or relations are assumed as original, and then consciousness is approached as a problem. "How did consciousness spring up in the universal machine?" This becomes the most baffling of mysteries. I affirm that this mystery is purely artificial and grows out of assuming an inadequate base of reference. For "matter," "thing," and "relation" are creatively constructed notions and by no means originally given material. On the contrary, consciousness is original and is presupposed in the very power to recognize and formulate a problem. There is something sterile in speculation concerning that which is eternally outside consciousness. Just as light can never comprehend darkness, for the simple reason that darkness vanishes as light penetrates it, so too the unconscious vanishes as consciousness pierces it. Thus every element that is brought into any speculation is, of necessity, within the field of consciousness. The eternally unconscious is indistinguishable, at any rate, from absolute nothingness, if it is not identical with it. It simply *is not* for any practical or valid theoretical purpose. This much we know, even though we know nothing else, "Consciousness is." For it is presupposed even in the acknowledgement of ignorance and in the agnostical and skeptical attitudes. But while every man is a living demonstration to himself that "consciousness is," not every man has realized that "consciousness-without-an-object is." The radical element in my philosophic departure inheres in the "without-an-object." Herein lies precisely the difference between a state of consciousness that is only relative or saturated in raw immediacy and no more, and one that involves profound mystical realization. However, consciousness is the common denominator underlying the possibility of any philosophy, world view, religious attitude, art, or science. I, therefore, affirm the systematic primacy of consciousness as such.

As soon as consciousness is concerned with objects, inter-relations, and other complexities are introduced and accordingly, all sorts of divergencies. Deleting content, only Consciousness-without-an-object remains as the common denominator. If approached in a purely theoretical spirit, this might have merely the value of an abstraction. I have demonstrated its actuality as a direct realization, but found it the most difficult of all things to attain when starting from the basis of reflective consciousness. However, when realized, it is the simplest of all things. When I say that Consciousness-without-an-object is, I imply its independence and self-existence. Everything else may be only a symbol. Problems concerning the genesis of specific symbols may become very difficult and require all the resources of highly trained capacity. But Consciousness-without-an-object is an unshakable base, and thus is an assurance transcending both unverifiable faith and relative knowledge.

As I assert the dependency of all contents upon Consciousness-without-an-object, so likewise do I affirm the concomitant dependency of the Self and all selves, because the existence of a self implies the existence of objects, whether subtle or gross, and as well, the existence of objects implies the presence of a self that is aware of them. The object and the self are polar existences that are interdependent. The notion of a self that is conscious without being conscious of anything does not correspond to any possible actuality. The object may be very abstract, such as a bare field of consciousness viewed as an object, but analysis will always reveal a polar relationship. The subject is the inverse or complement of the object, or in other words, its "other." Thus, for example, the object is the totality of all possible experience, and this is manifestly multiform and heterogeneous. In contrast, the pure self, conceived as the polarized power *to be aware*, is unitary and homogeneous. Taken in abstraction, the object, as such, is not a universe, but simply a multitude without interconnection and therefore not even a collection. The *uni*verse is the resultant of the interaction of the self and its object— that is, a disconnected multiplicity integrated through the unity of the self.

The technique of the higher Yoga would seem to imply the isolation of bare subjectivity as Self-consciousness totally devoid of content. The real meaning of this technique is, however, a shifting of the focus of consciousness *toward* bare subjectivity and away from objectivity, with the goal being in the nature of a limit that may be approached with unrestricted closeness of approximation, but that is never actually attained as long as any self remains. Fully to attain the goal is to destroy the subject as well as the object, and then there remains pure Consciousness-without-an-object—a state which is equally pure Consciousness-without-a-subject. But so long as the movement is toward pure subjectivity, the goal is unattainable, just as the last term of an infinite converging series is never reached through a step-by-step process.

The aspirant to Yoga starts with consciousness operating in the universe of experience and thought, and in a state of a self entangled with objects. This is the familiar state of human consciousness. The entanglement with objects leads to the superposition upon the self of qualities properly belonging to the objects alone. This state is akin to that of hypnosis, and is real bondage—the great cause of suffering. The first steps in Yoga technique have the significance of progressive disentanglement of the self and of dehypnotizing the consciousness. The process is one of radical dissociation of the self from objects. At the completion of the first stage the self stands opposed to and other than the universe of objects. Objects, now, are simply witnessed as something outside, and the identification is dissolved. This stage may be represented by the judgment, "I am other than that"—the "that" referring to all possible objects. The second stage is ushered in by a radical readjustment in which the self shifts to another plane or base, where relations vanish and the self is realized as identical with content of consciousness. Superficially, this may seem like a recurrence of the original participation or entanglement, but such is not the case as there has been a shift of base. The content of consciousness now is the inverse of that with which the aspirant originally started. The difference may be suggested by conceiving all objects in the original state as being vortices, or voids in a supersensuous and continuous plenum. The consciousness with which the Yoga process starts is exclusively aware of the vortices, or voids, the whole world of supposed things—while the culminating consciousness, thus far, functions in the supersensuous plenum. That plenum is realized

as the Self identical with content of consciousness—
the state consistently reported by the mystics. It is as
though the 'I', which in the original state was like a
bare point within the universe and circumscribed by
objects, had suddenly transformed itself into a space
that comprehended all objects. But there still remains
a self that is aware, that maintains its own identity,
and may be said to have a content that is the inverse
of experience; for such a self certainly realizes values
such as bliss, peace, and freedom. The more familiar
name for this State is Nirvana.

Most of the literature on the subject represents
Nirvana as the final culmination, but this is an error.
Nirvana is simply the inverse of the universe—thus
not the ultimate transcendence of the pairs of opposites. There is a still more advanced stage in Yoga. To
facilitate understanding of this stage it may help if we
review the significance of the first step, considered as
an affective transformation. In affective terms, the first
step is frequently called a renunciation of the universe,
i.e., the breaking of all attachment to objects. The
successful accomplishment of the first step brings a
very great reward, that is, consciousness operative in a
subjective or inverse sense. The realization here is extremely attractive, but attractiveness implies a self that
remains identical and that is still influenced by valuation. Now, the final stage of Yoga involves the renunciation of Nirvana, and that means the renunciation
of all attractiveness and reward. Such a renunciation
implies the final annulment of all claims of a self that
remains in any sense unique. Both consciousness as
object and consciousness as subject are now annulled.
There remains simply Consciousness-without-an-object,
which, in turn, comprehends both the universe and
Nirvana as potentialities. This stage is the culmination
of Yoga.

Modern physics and astronomy have developed a speculative conception that is, in some respects, an inverse reflection of the view elaborated here. This interpretation is derived from certain facts that have come to light in recent decades, partly as the result of the development of instrumental aids to observation and partly as the result of progress in interpretative theory. It now appears, quite clearly, that the older conception of matter as being composed of unchanging and indestructible atoms does not faithfully interpret the facts derived through experience.[1] It has become necessary to conceive of the atom as composed of still finer units, such as electrons, protons, positrons, and so forth, and these in turn as being subject to transformation under the appropriate conditions. When the transformation takes place it appears that ponderable matter assumes a state of radiant energy. This process, seemingly, is proceeding in the stars continuously and is the source of the energy derived from them upon the surface of the earth. Apparently, then, the stars are disintegrating in the sense that matter concentrated in bodies at widely separated points in space is being transformed into radiant energy which spreads throughout all space. All this suggests that the various systems of stars will ultimately disappear as masses of ponderable matter, and in their place will be a space uniformly filled with radiant energy. On the other hand, observation of numerous extragalactic nebulae suggests, very convincingly, that both stars and systems of stars are generated by an aggregation of more or less homogeneous and amorphous matter into concentrated and more or less organized form. These various facts from observation, combined with theory, suggest the following conclusions:

a. That if the history of the stellar universe were

traced back far enough in time we would find a stage wherein there were no stars, but only a more or less homogeneous matter and radiation spread uniformly throughout space.[2]

b. That if we could follow the life of the systems of stars far enough into the future, we would come to a time when most matter, if not all, would be reduced or transformed into radiation extending throughout space.

c. That the two notions of conservation of mass and of energy must be united into the conception of a persistent Energy which may appear in the forms either of ponderable mass or of field energy, the latter including that which is termed radiation.

The above conceptions leave us with but one constant or "invariant," i.e., Energy, which may appear at certain times as ponderable matter, and at others as transformed into the state of radiant energy.[3] If now we substitute for "Consciousness-without-an-object" the notion of "Energy"; for the "Universe"—in the sense of all objects—the notion of "ponderable matter"; and for "Nirvana," the notion of "state of radiation," we can restate our first aphorisms as follows:

1 ... *Energy is.*

2 ... *Before ponderable matter was, Energy is.*

3 ... *Though ponderable matter seems to exist,*
Energy is.

4 ... *When ponderable matter vanishes,*
yet remaining through all unaffected, Energy is.

5 . . . Outside of Energy there is no matter.

11 . . . Within Energy lie
both ponderable matter and radiant energy,
yet for Energy these two are the same.[4]

This physical conception has a high order of theoretical beauty, and I regard it as one of the finer products of scientific art. It effects a very great conceptual simplification, and enables us to picture a wide range of transformation in nature as experienced within the organization of an essentially simple unifying concept. However, what we have is a construction of the creative intellect, in part operating upon a material given through observation, and in part conditioning the observation. We have no right to say that this theory, or any modification that may take place in the future, is nature as it is apart from the consciousness of all thinkers. Any question of the truth or reality-value of the theory must be judged in relationship to a conscious thinker. Further, we have no right to assert dogmatically that, even though for our science this theory should prove to be ultimately valid, then it must necessarily be valid for any competent thinker whatsoever. In fact, it is entirely possible, nay more, quite probable, that the scientists of an entirely different culture, although of comparable capacity and supplied with comparable resources for investigation, would none the less construct an entirely different theoretical structure for the organization of their corresponding experience. Yet, this would not discredit the relative validity of the foregoing theory for our present culture.

The value of a theory or of any conceptual formulation lies in the fact that it gives the intelligent consciousness a basis for orienting itself and for achieving either purposive control of, or intelligent understanding in, the sea of existences. In the strictly metaphysical sense, i.e., in the sense that is not related to any concrete thinker, no conceptual formulation is either true or false. It is simply irrelevant. Nor, on the other hand, can experience prove the truth or falsity of any fundamental theory, though it can check the various derivative theories.[5]

If we regard the fundamental theories—the original bases or starting points—as only assumptions, then the whole of science is grounded in uncertainty and affords no security. But if the fundamental theories are grounded in insight—a mystical function—then it is valid for science to proceed with a basic assurance that is essentially of the same type as that attained through mystical awakening. All of which simply means that science, completely divorced from the religious spirit, is no more than sterile formalism. In point of fact, much of our science is far from sterile, but then there is actually much real religion in it. This factor should be given a larger theoretical recognition and its significance should be more adequately appreciated.

It is not difficult to see that the fundamental theories of science are of the nature of consciousness, since their existence is, for us, in thought alone—and a conscious thought at that. But such theories contain terms pointing to referents that in some sense have an objective existence. At first, one may be disposed to think that these referents must lie outside consciousness. However, it can easily be shown that even here we have actually drawn upon no material from beyond consciousness, though it lies or rests in another compartment of consciousness as contrasted to that of the interpretative theory. We can illustrate this by reference to what is one of the most objective notions of all physical science. This is the notion of "mass."[6]

When we ask, "What is mass?" we find that it is, in effect, defined in two ways, as follows:

1. Mass is measured by inertia in the field of a force.

2. Mass is measured by weight in the gravitational field of a standard piece of matter, i.e., the earth.

"Inertia" is the name given to the resistance that a body opposes to an effort ('force') to speed up its motion or to retard its motion. "Weight" is the name for the effort ('force') required to hold a body against the so-called force of gravity. But what do we mean by resistance and effort? Here we step out of the conceptual system into the realm of data from experience. Resistance and effort are sensory experiences, particularly involving the kinesthetic sense. Thus, at least in so far as man is concerned, both of these 'forces' are existences in consciousness. To predicate that they correspond to existences outside of and independent of, consciousness in every sense is to create a speculative dogma that in the very nature of the case can never be verified. For verification operates only within the field of consciousness. This is simply another instance of the principle that consciousness can never know absolute unconsciousness, for where consciousness is, unconsciousness is not. Undoubtedly, speculative theory can proceed upon the assumption that there are existences outside consciousness in every sense, but this is the assumption of an "as if" that can never be verified, either mystically or in any other way. The assumption may have a relative value, but it lacks all authority, and properly, may not be invoked to oppose the rational right of anybody to refuse to accept it.

We know immediately that consciousness is; but we do not know that mass is, immediately. All that we do know concerning the latter is that systematic constructions involving the concept of mass can be produced that give to man a greater command over nature and establish a greater harmony between conscious man and the apparent environment in which he finds himself. Yet both of these are values within consciousness.[7]

From the basis of Consciousness-without-an-object there is no necessity of predicating absolutely unconscious existences. There would remain a distinction to be drawn between different kinds and levels of consciousness, and in particular, the distinction between consciousness that is not conscious of itself and consciousness that is conscious of itself. This leaves plenty of room for the existence of something beyond "consciousness-which-is-conscious-of-itself," or "self-consciousness," and thus there can be a flow into and out of the field of reflective consciousness. This, I submit, is all that science needs to interpret the fractional character of the data from experience. In addition, the view I am offering eliminates the question: How is it possible for that which is wholly outside consciousness, in every sense, to enter consciousness? Primeval Consciousness is the all in all, and only self-consciousness grows.

While it is a theoretical impossibility for consciousness to comprehend that which is absolutely outside consciousness, in every sense, there is no theoretical barrier that stands in the way of self-consciousness spreading out in Primeval Consciousness without limit, for self-consciousness is composed of the very stuff of consciousness itself. An extending comprehension of Primeval Consciousness by self-consciousness is simply a case of light assimilating Light. The Light cannot know darkness, because where light goes the darkness vanishes, but light can, in principle, know the light as it is of its own nature.

Opposed to consciousness as the only existence there stands the counter notion of voidness. In this sense the void is a somewhat that is not, or has no substance. Now, without voids there would be nothing within the Primeval Plenum of Consciousness to arouse self-consciousness into action. The voids may be regarded as zones of tension wherein consciousness negates itself and thus blanks itself out in greater or less degree. Such voids have the value of disturbance in the primeval equilibrium. We may regard this disturbance as acting like an irritant that tends to arouse consciousness to an awareness of itself. It is an instance of *absence* arousing the power to be aware of *presence*. Here, then, we have a basis afforded for interpreting evolutionary development. Instead of that development being a means whereby consciousness is finally evolved out of the mechanical processes of dead nature, we have a progressive unfoldment of self-consciousness within a matrix of Primeval Consciousness. The play and interplay of voids, instead of atoms of an external and dead matter, are the background of the universe of objects. The voids arouse attention within consciousness simply because of their pain-value. The focusing power aroused by attention in time becomes self-consciousness, or the power to be conscious of consciousness. The multiform combinations of the voids produce all the configurations of experience and thought, and these in turn have the value of symbols, which in the last analysis are of instrumental value only. The symbols indicate a preexistent and formless Meaning. When, for any individual center of consciousness,[8] the Meaning can be assimilated directly without the instrumentality of the symbols, then for that individual the evolution of consciousness within the field of consciousness of objects has been completed. But until that time symbols are necessary.

Now we are in a position to see the metaphysical function of science. It is concerned with the progressive development of a system of symbols, the raw material of which is given through experience. Science —at any rate in the sense of physical science—is not concerned with a study of actual existences. Its raw material consists of voids or absences. These are formed into a system of relations that has value in expanding self-consciousness and in forming a symbol of hidden Meaning. So, from the standpoint of this philosophy, the work of the scientists is quite valid, regardless of the form of the working hypotheses employed. The only point where this view could come into conflict with the thought of any individual scientist would arise in the case where the latter superimposes an extrascientific interpretation upon the material with which he works and upon his conclusions. The technical functions of science do not require that its materials should be a substantial existence. They only require that that material should fit into an intelligible system of relations.

The most fundamental principle of this philosophy is that consciousness, as such, is original and primary, and thus not merely an attribute of something else. But as here understood, "consciousness" is not a synonym of "spirit," since, generally, the spiritual or idealistic philosophies have regarded "spirit" as primary and represented consciousness as an attribute of spirit. This leaves the possibility that spirit, in some phase of its total character, may be unconscious, so that consciousness is reduced to a partial and derivative aspect. Let this be clear, that here it is not predicated that any spiritual or other kind of being is primary. On the contrary, Consciousness *is*, before any being *became*. Thus, "God," whether considered as an existence or simply as an integrating concept, is, in any case, derivative. We may properly view certain levels of consciousness, which transcend the human form of consciousness, as Divine. All terms derived from the notion of Divinity certainly have a very high order of psychological significance, at the very least, and I do make use of them. But I do not regard them as corresponding to the most ultimate values.

It seems to be in accord with well-established philosophical usage to regard "spirit" as having the same connotation as either the "Self" or "God." Following this custom we may say, when consciousness of objects is born, spirit also is born as the complemental or subjective principle. Objects being taken as the equivalent of matter, then spirit and matter stand as interdependent notions. Neither of these is possible without the other, though spirit may be regarded as positive, while matter is negative.

To predicate that consciousness is original and self-existent does not imply that *Being* is dependent upon *being known*. For while cognition is a mode of consciousness, it is not identical with consciousness. Thus affective and conative states are essentially noncognitive, though they are part and parcel of consciousness. I predicate that pure consciousness is the self-existent antecedent of all these modes of ordinary states of consciousness, also of the less familiar mystical states, and likewise of the forms of consciousness characteristic of nonhuman beings. On the other hand, "to know" does *imply* being, but the implication is of an antecedent, not of a consequent. To become aware of knowing is to become aware of the reality—in this case relative reality—of Being. The awareness of this reality is something achieved, but the achievement has not made the reality. However, *to be known* is to *exist*, and this is a true sequential or derivative existence. Being is *antecedent*, existence *derivative*.

To be known is to be an object. Since by "universe" I mean the totality of all possible objects, it then follows that the universe is dependent upon being known for its *existence*. The universe exists for one who experiences or thinks, but for none other. Even the Naturalist, who predicates the existence of *things* apart from all consciousness, actually is dealing with a notion that exists only in his consciousness. He has not arrived at something that lies outside consciousness, and only fools himself when he imagines that he has done so. Knowing is a Light that drives away the darkness, and thus forever fails to comprehend darkness. It is useless to predicate existence in the darkness of total and unresolvable unconsciousness, in every sense, for it is an absolute impossibility to verify any such predication. Such a predication is not only unphilosophic, it is, as well, unscientific, for science requires of all hypotheses that they shall be capable of verification. In fact, science even goes further than the mystic and requires that the verification must be of a type that falls within the range of the modes of consciousness of the ordinary nonmystical man. Thus the scientist who blossoms as a naturalistic philosopher violates his own scientific canons in the most violent manner. It is at this point that the Idealist is rigorous in his methodology, and not the so-called scientific philosopher.

All *things* exist as objects, and only so. Especially is this true for him who experiences or thinks. To anesthetize the powers of experiencing and thinking is to destroy the universe, but this does not imply the annihilation of consciousness in the Gnostic sense. Consciousness remains in the Nirvanic State. If self-consciousness has been developed to that degree of strength such that it can persist in the face of the process of anesthetizing, then the resultant is an awakening to realization of the Nirvanic State, otherwise this State is like dreamless sleep. But dreamless sleep is to be regarded simply as a state of consciousness where self-consciousness—that is, consciousness that is conscious of itself—is unawakened. All men are in Nirvana in the hinterland of their consciousness. The Nirvani, in the technical sense, differs essentially from the ordinary man only in that he has carried self-consciousness over into the hinterland.

Here I am introducing nothing that cannot be verified, for, by taking the appropriate steps, men can actually take self-consciousness across into the hinterland. Admittedly, this is not easy to do. It involves a good deal more than the process of verification adequate for the checking of ordinary scientific hypotheses. But it has been done. I have done it, and I find there is an abundant literature furnishing the testimony of others who have claimed to have done so. This literature springs up at all periods, as far as we have historic records, and through it all there is a common thread of meaning underlying a wide range of more or less incompatible overbelief. Representative men of all cultures, races, and creeds have supplied this common testimony. They agree with respect to a certain consciousness-quale and that the basis of this consciousness was direct, individual realization, transcending both faith and authority. Thus, in the present thesis, there is no violation of the scientific demand that a judgment of actuality or reality must be capable of verification. But the verification does require going beyond the ordinary modes of consciousness, and thus does transcend the secondary requirement of western physical science. However, this secondary requirement restricts our science to a delimited field and is of only pragmatic value so long as it cannot be proved that the ordinary modes of human consciousness are the only modes there possibly can be. No such proof exists, nor can it be made, for the most that any man could possibly say is that, so far, he, individually, has found no other ways of consciousness; and that proves nothing concerning consciousness *per se*.

Modern psychology distinguishes between objects that it calls real and objects that it calls hallucinations. From the standpoint of Consciousness-without-an-object there is no important difference between these two sets of objects. The so-called real objects are experienced by groups of men in common, while the hallucinations are generally private. This is merely a social criterion of reality and has no logical force. Essentially it is as meaningless as determining physical laws by popular vote. Doubtless, if a Newton, with all his insight and intellectual power unimpaired, were transplanted to the environment of a primitive society and judged by his milieu, he would be regarded as a fool whose consciousness was filled with hallucinations. The social judgment of reality would be against him. Our society has reached a level where it can verify the insight of Newton, in considerable degree, but the validity of that insight exists independently of the social power to verify it. All of which simply means that the fact that objects exist for a given individual *privately* is not sufficient either to credit them with reality or to discredit them by calling them unreal hallucinations. The problem of reality is not to be handled in any such simple offhand manner. In fact, such a method is sheer intellectual tyranny. It is entirely possible that society, and not the individual man, is the greater fool. I am inclined to think so.

Objects, whether of the common social type or the so-called hallucinations, exist for the powers of experiencing and thinking, and thus both are derivative. If by "Reality" we mean the nonderivative, then both types of objects are unreal. In the narrower or pragmatic sense, the one type of object may be more real than the other, when taken in relation to a given purpose. It may well be that in the narrow sense of the purpose of western physical science, the social object is more real, but from the religious standpoint, in certain instances at any rate, the reverse valuation is far more likely to be true. But here we have no more than valuation with respect to specific purpose.

Some mystical states, probably the greater number, involve the experiencing of subtle objects of the type that the psychologist calls hallucination. Practically, this has the effect of classifying the mystic with the psychotic, apparently with the intent of common depreciation. Such a course involves both intellectual laziness and a failure in discrimination. Since a "hallucination" merely means private experience as opposed to social experience, it constitutes no true judgment of value. There is often a world of difference between one and another so-called hallucination. The difference between the state of consciousness of a drunkard, enjoying delirium tremens, and that of a seer like Swedenborg, is as far apart as the poles. All too often the psychologist calls both merely states of hallucination, and acts as though he thought that by giving a name he had solved the whole problem. As a matter of fact, the real problem here is one of valuation, just as it is with the social objects. The vital question in either case is: How far and on what level do the objects arouse the realization of Meaning? The objects that do this in higher degree and on a higher level may properly be regarded as possessing the greater relative reality. Thus, in a given case, the so-called hallucination may far outreach any social object in the relative reality. In any case, the type of the object, whether social or private, is not by itself, any measure of its value or reality. Neither type has nonderivative Reality or Meaning.

That in some sense the *Object* exists cannot be denied, for it is unquestionably a datum for immediate experience. But to affirm further that the *Thing* exists is to add an overbelief that is not necessary for either experience or reason. As these terms are here employed, the "Object" is to be regarded as always a content of consciousness, and thus implies a relationship to or within consciousness. In contrast, the "Thing" is that which is *supposed* to exist, quite independently of any relationship to or within consciousness. Thus the Thing is to be regarded as a sort of thing-in-itself that stands apart from any dependent relationship to consciousness as a source of its existence. It is not the present purpose to attempt to prove that a self-existent thing is impossible but simply that the supposition of its existence is neither practically nor theoretically necessary, and also that its existence cannot be demonstrated.

That the existence of the Thing cannot be demonstrated is very easily shown. For demonstration never gives us anything but an existence, a relationship, a value, and so forth, for consciousness. Hence, that which is demonstrated to be is already a content for consciousness, and therefore, an object. Unquestionably, new and unpredictable contents can enter *empiric* consciousness. To assume that the sudden arising of the new contents implies an existence wholly independent of consciousness, in every sense, that merely happened to enter into relationship with consciousness, may be natural enough. But for logic this assumption is not necessary, and by hypothesis, it cannot be empirically verified. For, so far as experience and logic can determine to the contrary, it is as readily thinkable that when the new content of consciousness arose it actually, then, came into existence for the first time. No doubt, the notion of the birth of an existence quite *de novo* or *ex nihilo* is repugnant to the deepseated conviction that all existences are traceable to causal antecedents. But, whatever validity may attach to this conviction, it yet remains something other than a derivation from either experience or logic. That it is not a derivation from experience has already been well established by the critical analysis of David Hume, and accordingly, further discussion of this point is not necessary here. That it is not a derivation from pure logic is also clear, as we now understand quite well that logic supplies only the formal implications of the given material upon which it operates. The innate material of logic, itself, consists only of the original logical constants, and since the notion that every existence must have a causal antecedent is not one of these, it follows that this notion is neither a prerequisite of logic nor a consequence to be derived from logical process alone.

There remains the question of the claim imposed by the conviction that there is no existence that does not have an adequate causal antecedent, i.e., that no existence can be *ex nihilo* or *de novo*. I assume the validity of the claim of this conviction as a component part of consciousness, which is not derived either from logic or experience. The question then arises: Does this conviction require that the antecedent of a newly arisen object in relative consciousness shall be a thing existing independently of consciousness in every sense? The answer is no, since another adequate source is thinkable, and in addition, has already become a working hypothesis of Analytic Psychology. We can conceive of the antecedent of the newly arisen object as lying in the psychologic unconscious. This interpretation is already commonly employed in Analytic Psychology in the exposition of the aetiology of the phantasy products of introversion. In the case of the phantasy function, objects do appear suddenly from a hidden matrix, either in ideal or sensible form. Analytic Psychology has found it unnecessary to assume a causal antecedent of such objects in terms of things existing independently of the psyche in every sense. To extend this aetiology to the objects of the objective senses involves no logical or empiric difficulty, and merely extends a principle of explanation with radical consistency.

It may be objected that in introducing the notion of the psychological unconscious as the causal antecedent of the newly arisen object we have merely substituted a logical equivalent of the Thing, existing independently of consciousness in every sense. But this is not so. For, as has been shown already at some length, the psychological unconscious does not imply unconsciousness in every sense. It is merely that which is unconscious to ordinary waking consciousness, which is quite different from saying that it is unconscious with respect to consciousness in every sense. For it is clear that consciousness that is not conscious of itself is indistinguishable from unconsciousness. Philosophically, then, it is possible to affirm the exclusive existence of all objects and their antecedents in consciousness and yet employ the notion of the unconscious in the *psychological* sense.

From the foregoing it should be clear that the demonstration of the existence of the independent Thing is impossible. At the same time, in the latter part of the above argument, it has been shown that its existence is not a necessary assumption for logic, experience, or the conviction that every existence must have an adequate causal antecedent. For I have suggested a thinkable aetiology that supplies what is necessary, and yet dispenses with the notion of a thing existing independently of consciousness, in every sense. This completes the formal argument. Let us now examine the extralogical considerations that may bear upon this proposed aetiology.

The requirements of a physical science are fundamentally simple. Chief among these are the following. (*a*) The objective content of the science must be of such a nature that it can be perceived by the objective senses, either directly or indirectly, through the intervention of instruments, and these senses must be exclusively those that are active in the typical representative of our culture, or of the human race. (*b*) This material becomes a science when, and only when, it has become organized into a rationally thinkable system that possesses internal coherence and that, in addition, makes possible the prediction of future objective events in such a way as to render either observational or experimental checking possible. These are the two principal requirements of a pure physical science. Applied science requires, in addition, that the organization of the raw material of a science shall be such that, at least, some degree of practical control of the object is achieved. Any theory as to the real nature of the objects that form the content of a science, that does not interfere with the action of these fundamental requirements of science, leaves to science the full freedom that science qua science can claim. If the behavior of the Object were wholly arbitrary or irrational in every sense, no science, pure or applied, could ever be possible. A science is possible only to the extent that the perceived object can enter into some relationship with a rationally thinkable system. It is not necessary that such a system shall be the only conceivable one or that it shall be the ultimately true or complete system. The objective of physical science is partial. (*a*) It does not aim to comprehend the totality of all possible knowledge. This is evident from the fact that it arbitrarily excludes all material that cannot be perceived directly or indirectly through the objective senses of the typical representative of our culture or our humanity. Thus, such material of consciousness as there may be that is available only through other doors or by other modes of consciousness is extrascientific—in the western sense—however much such material may be an object for knowledge. (*b*) It does not include in its structure those modes or aspects of consciousness that are not to be classed as knowledge of objective content. Thus Self-knowledge or the feeling of Love are not part of the *structure* of any physical science.

In contrast to the specialized demands of a physical science, philosophy has for its field all possible aspects of consciousness. It is concerned with the religious, ethical, and aesthetic values, just as truly as with the general problems that are vital to the existence of science. Further, its concern with the general problems of physical science is not greater then with the similar problems of any other possible type of science. That the existence of sciences other than physical science is more than an academic possibility is revealed by the development of the psychologies *with a psyche*.[9] However, philosophy overlaps the motif of physical science in that it seeks a systematic objective.

All philosophies fail that do not take into account every conceivable possibility of consciousness and also grant to every possibility full freedom in its proper domain. The current schools of philosophy, known as Naturalism, Neorealism, and Pragmatism, have granted to natural science full recognition. In so far as the ethical problem is conceived as a matter of social relationship, Pragmatism has made valuable contributions to ethical theory and interpretation. But all these philosophies fail—some of them completely—to give adequate recognition to the necessities of the religious and mystical states of consciousness. They are, therefore, valuable only as partial philosophies. Much of consciousness-value they either ignore or treat with an unacceptable coercion. They are all psychologically one-sided. They represent, either exclusively or predominantly, the extroverted attitude in individual or social psychology. They either neglect entirely the values that are immediately apparent to the introverted attitude, or they treat such values with the condescension of extroverted pride that is quite unacceptable to any well-developed introvert. On the other hand, the systems of philosophy classified under Idealism, while they give with greater or less adequacy recognition of the introvert and the religious and mystical values, yet they have failed with respect to the extroverted standpoint. Since these four types of philosophic system cover the ground of western philosophic contribution, we must conclude that the West has not yet produced the adequate philosophic statement.

Why is it that the western mind so predominantly

attributes the reality-value to the material that is the peculiar concern of physical science? It is not simply because that material is given as objectively sensible. Ordinary phantasy often produces objects that are sensibly apparent, yet commonly these objects are considered to be unreal. It is not due to the fact that the material of science lends itself to a logically systematic statement. There are mathematical systems grounded upon freely created fundamental assumptions that have the character of logically coherent, systematic wholes. However, these are not commonly considered to be possessed of reality-value. It does not inhere in a positive demonstration that science deals with a knowledge of existent things independent of all consciousness as such, as has already been shown. There seems to be but one fact of experience that affords the explanation of this attribution of reality-value to the material of physical science and that is that this material is relatively common and constant with respect to the vast majority of observers, and that so far as is commonly known, no individual can successfully act as though this material were not. Here there seems to be an objective somewhat with which the conscious being must come to terms if he is so to adapt his life as to live successfully.

Certainly, there is something or somewhat, in some sense, with which the individual must make terms. But this fact by no means implies that that something or somewhat is an independent self-existent reality. For we can give it an interpretation that, while independent self-existence is denied of it, yet retains for it its conditioning character with respect to the functioning of conscious beings. We may regard it as a collective phantasy projected from the collective unconscious and possessing a relatively frozen or fixed form, which, in turn, is but a measure of the stability of the collective unconscious. This would give to the projected phantasy the characteristic of being an objective determinant, and thus it is easy to understand why it should have acquired the seeming of primary reality-value.

Is there any respect in which the above interpretation of the objective somewhat would be incompatible with the facts of experience? There seems to be no objection that will stand after examination. The objective material of consciousness is given through the senses and only through the senses. But the senses supply merely the forms of one of the functions of consciousness, namely that of sensation. Here we are forever confined to material that is reducible to sensation, save in so far as material from other functions of consciousness are added to it. Much material that has an objective appearance is given in ordinary phantasy, even though it is the general judgment that such appearance is not an objective existence-in-itself. By the technique of hypnotism, similar appearances have been produced in the consciousness of the subject through suggestion. Here, again, there is no question of a corresponding objective thing that is an independent existence-in-itself. Give to such an hypnoidal appearance the character of being a collective component of all human consciousness, and then we may ask: In what way would it be distinguishable from the material acquired by ordinary extroverted observation? It would seem that every possibility of natural science that now exists would still remain. The significance of the scientific product, alone, would be changed. But this level of significance-evaluation lies outside the domain of scientific determination, as such, and thus there would be no interference with the freedom of natural science in the field or sector of consciousness available to it.

We should be forced to interpret the facts and laws

of science as being purely psychical existence, though of an order of relative stability. The laws, as well as the facts, would have their real abiding place in the psychological collective unconscious.

I believe this philosophy allows to science all requisite freedom to develop in its own dimension. The interpretation of the significance of its facts, processes, and products, alone, is changed. I merely challenge the pretended right of the scientist to hypostatize the material of his science into a supposedly substantial and independent Thing. With the abandonment of this hypostasis, there falls all right to the claim of any peculiar reality-value attaching to the object of science or of sensation in general. There remains a relative or pragmatic reality-value that has validity within the restricted sector of consciousness involved, but only that. In a word, the accusation that a given content of consciousness has a phantasy-origin would no longer, by itself, be sufficient to establish inferior reality-value, as compared with the products of physical science, since this too rests upon essentially the same ground. Thus the argument that serves to undermine the reality of religious or mystical hypostasis would be a two-edged sword that likewise undermines the reality of scientific or sensuous hypostasis. Thus far, the content of mystical insight would have a right to claim reality-value that is not inferior to that which the scientist or extroverted consciousness may claim for his material. In a word, the extrovert must renounce his arrogant claim to peculiar possession of the sense for reality. He is oriented to a sector of relative reality, and only that. It is by no means evident that this sector ultimately releases the greater power. At any rate, this question becomes an open one.

A vital consequence of the present thesis is that, if there is any power that can consciously operate upon the psychological collective unconscious, then that power would be superior to any of the products of phantasy, whether religious or scientific. For it would be a power acting upon the root-source of all contents of consciousness of whatever nature. Theoretically, such a power would have the capacity of causing all the material of objective perception, as well as of religious phantasy, to vanish or to be transformed through processes that could not be objectively traced. Such a power, it must be understood, does not imply the capacity to destroy consciousness as such, but simply to destroy, or rather, transform, all content. It should also be clear that such a power would lie closer to ultimate Reality than any of the content of consciousness over which it has mastery.

The practical question is: Does such a power exist? So far, at least, I do not find it possible to give an objectively satisfactory answer to this question. To my own satisfaction I have verified its existence, but I do not find it possible to do more than build a more or less satisfactory presumption for its existence, with respect to empiric centers of consciousness other than my own. It seems that there is a Transcendent Somewhat that must be sampled, at least, to be known. While I do affirm the reality of this Transcendent Somewhat and the existence of a conscious Power that can operate upon the collective unconscious of psychology, I do not claim the capacity to coerce recognition of either.

The term "Universe" is here employed with the connotation of the Buddhist term "Sangsara." Thus I do not confine the meaning of "Universe" to the totality of all objects of ordinary waking consciousness. It includes, as well, the so-called hallucinations, dream states, and any other possible states of consciousness during physical life or after death in which there is consciousness of objects. Opposed to this is the Nirvanic state of consciousness in which there are no objects, for the simple reason that in that State there is no subject-object relationship. Thus, Nirvanic Consciousness is not identical with the totality of all mystical states of consciousness, but on the contrary is the culminating point of the mystical Path into the *subjective pole* of consciousness. Only a few, even among the mystics, have gone this far, to judge from the available records. It follows that there are mystical states that do not transcend Sangsara, and in general, such are the more understandable to objective consciousness.

But the further the mystic goes in his penetration to subjective deeps, the less he can say in terms that are intelligible to ordinary consciousness, when trying to report the value of his realization. The higher the point of attainment, the less effective does concrete sensuous imagery become as a symbol of its value. Abstract concepts remain as effective symbols longer, but in any case all that can be said is of value only as a symbol. This is necessarily so, since the representation must be in terms of objects, whether sensory or conceptual, whereas the actuality is not an object. A so-called hallucination or phantasy may, in a given case, supply a truer symbol than one formed out of the material of social experience, though this is not necessarily so. In any case, the vital point is that from the standpoint of Nirvanic Consciousness everything supplied by the Universe or Sangsara is of symbolic or instrumental significance only. At this point I am in accord with the epistemology of the Pragmatists, but I go further than any Pragmatist with whom I am familiar, for I regard all experience, as well as intellection, as being, in the last analysis, of only instrumental value, and even regard experience as no more than a catalytic agent, valuable as an arouser of self-consciousness.

It is only recently that western scholarship has begun to come to an intelligent understanding of the state of consciousness called "Nirvana." Recent translations of authentic northern Buddhist canonical literature should go far in the clarification of the older misconceptions. The etymology of the term "Nirvana" is unfortunate. To be 'blown-out' naturally does seem like total annihilation. But this is a great misconception. A truer understanding is reached by regarding the Nirvanic State as that realized when the powers of experiencing and thinking are anesthetized *without destroying self-consciousness*. It is a *way* of consciousness that is blown-out, not consciousness per se. To understand the idea in a form that is at all valid, it is necessary to think of all form or objects and all structures of thought and in consciousness, in general, as being in the nature of limitations imposed upon the play of consciousness. Remove the limitations, while holding to self-consciousness, and the Nirvanic State is instantaneously realized. Since this is a freeing of consciousness from limitations, it has been traditionally called "Liberation." Thus 'Freedom' is the prime keynote of the State. But from this Freedom, when realized, affective and noetic values are precipitated. The latter, in some degree, can irradiate both thought and experience, and thus be an illuminating and blessing force within the universe. Consequently, Nirvana is a State of consciousness that can and does produce a difference of fact within the universe of experience. This is sufficient to give it pragmatic value. But this pragmatic value is merely a derivative and transformed value and thus of only partial significance.

A critical study of the use of the terms "Nirvana"

and "Moksha," in Buddhist and Hindu literature, reveals that the meaning intended is not always the same. At times one receives the impression that Nirvana is Absolute Consciousness, while at others one runs across a differentiation between different degrees or levels of Nirvanic Consciousness, and even the explicit statement that the Nirvanic State is not an absolute state. Clearly, some of the writers are stricter in their usage of the term than others. If we view the term as sometimes used to designate a genus, and at other times a species under that genus, the apparent incompatibility of usage is largely, if not wholly, clarified. The primary mark of the genus would be that it is a state of consciousness transcending the subject-object relationship, and therefore inevitably ineffable for relative consciousness. Differentiation of this genus into various species implies that within the consciousness transcending the subject-object relationship there are differences of level or phase, though these differences must remain unintelligible for the subject-object type of consciousness, as such.

At the time of the deeper level of Recognition that occurred to me spontaneously on the eighth of September, I was completely surprised. Up to that time I had found nothing in my readings that had suggested to me the existence of such a state. I named it, tentatively, from its affective quale, which had the quality of thoroughgoing indifference. It seemed to transcend Nirvana in the usual sense, since the latter is always represented as having the affective quale of supermundane Bliss. I had previously known such a State, but while on the level of the High Indifference, I realized Bliss as lying below me, as something that I could participate in or refrain from at will. Subsequent to the period of being immersed in the Higher State, while functioning on the level of subject-object consciousness, I was somewhat troubled lest I had made some error in my interpretation.[10] To check myself I made a search of the available literature, but I found no clear verification until I chanced upon the translation of Tibetan Buddhism, which Evans-Wentz has edited and published in English. Here I finally found the references in which the Primordial Consciousness, symbolized by the "Clear Light" and in other ways, is represented as the container of the Nirvanic as well as the Sangsaric State. This supplied a conceptual form that confirmed my own interpretation of the culminating stage of Recognition. It made clear, also, that "Nirvana," as sometimes employed, is made to include the "Clear Light," a state that is neither subjective nor objective, while in other connections it refers only to the purely subjective State. Finally, I developed the symbol of "Consciousness-without-an-object" as a representation with a meaning or reference analogous to, if not identical with, the "Clear Light," and thus was enabled to add a noetic designation to the affective one I had already found.

Consciousness-without-an-object is the keystone that completes the arch. It is the final step necessary to produce a self-contained system of consciousness. Nirvana stands as a phase of consciousness standing in contrapuntal relationship to the sum total of all Sangsaric states—the consciousness behind the Self that is focused upon objects. It is thus the 'other' of all consciousness of the subject-object type. But the predication or realization of any state and its other, in discrete stages, is not a complete cycle, for the two imply a mutual container. This mutual container is found in Consciousness-without-an-object, and this latter affords a base from which Nirvana, as well as Sangsara, falls into comprehensive perspective. Consciousness-without-an-object is neutral with respect to every polarity and thus in principle gives command over all polarities. It affords the basis for a philosophic integration that is neither introversive nor extroversive. This implies a philosophy that, as a whole, is neither idealistic, in the subjective sense, nor realistic, but which may incorporate both idealistic and realistic aspects. It should be equally acceptable to religious and scientific consciousness.

The actual working consciousness of man is not purely Sangsaric. Man's bondage to subject-object consciousness inheres in the fact that, characteristically, his analysis of consciousness has succeeded in capturing only the Sangsaric element. For most men the Nirvanic element moves in the darkness of the not-self-conscious, such as dreamless sleep. In our western philosophic analysis of relative consciousness we have always come ultimately to a blank wall, though even at that limit consciousness is found to be a stream. Whence this stream and whither? For ordinary subject-object consciousness the final answer is the Unknown and the Unknowable. But this is correct only for the type of consciousness in question. Consciousness in the sense of Gnosis can and has gone farther, driving the Unknown far back into the Transcendental Plenum. And who is there who can place a final theoretical limit on this recession of the Unknown?

The Nirvanic State is not far away, but near at hand, in fact closer than the universe of objects. There is no difference between the purely subjective element of the subject-object consciousness and Nirvana. And what is nearer to man than his most immediate Self, that which he calls 'I', and which is always present, however much the content of consciousness may change? Man has the power to see, yet he constantly projects himself into the objects seen, and complementarily, introjects the object into himself, thereby superimposing upon himself the limitations of those objects. Every human problem grows out of this, and the never-ending stream of unresolved or half-resolved problems cannot be eliminated until this vicious habit is broken. Every other relief is meliorative or palliative and no more. Mayhap melioration does more harm than good. I am often inclined to think so, for individual man might often try harder to escape from a trap that had become completely unendurable, and thus succeed in the resolution of the life problem more frequently than he does. Merely making the trap more endurable by melioration may well have the effect of delaying the crisis, and so result in an increase of the sum total of suffering. Let man so change the polarization of his self-analyzing consciousness that he may see his seeing, as it were, and at once, he breaks the participation in objects. Of course, this seeing of seeing is expressed in the language of subject-object consciousness, because we have no other language. In the actual seeing of seeing, the self and the object become identical.

When an individual has at last learned the trick of dissociating his 'I' or subject from the whole universe of objects, he has, seemingly, retreated into a bare point of consciousness. But the moment he succeeds in doing this, the point is metamorphosed into a kind of space in which the Self and the content of consciousness are blended in one inseparable whole. I have called this the Spatial Void. Now it must be understood that this is not a state wherein the individual merely finds himself *in* space, but he is, as a Self, identical with the whole of Space. It is not consciousness as functioning through bodies and aware of objects, but a subjective state dissociated from all bodies and not concerned with objects. Yet it would be incorrect to regard it as a purely homogeneous consciousness in the sense of a fixed state, totally devoid of variety. For consciousness and motion, in some sense, are inseparable.

To arrive at a symbolic concept that may fairly suggest motion in the Nirvanic sense, it is necessary to analyze motion in the universe of objects and then develop its inverse. The consciousness of objects is atomic. By this I mean that it is in the form of a series of discrete states or apprehensions, in the sense in which Kant spoke of the manifold given through experience. This is well illustrated by the cinematograph, where we actually have a series of still photographs thrown upon the screen in rapid succession. The spectator is not actually witnessing motion, but merely a series of still images. Only a fraction of the original drama was actually photographed. Yet the effect upon the spectator is very similar to that produced by original scenes enacted by living actors. Now, actually the camera reproduces essentially the process of visual seeing. A certain amount of time is required before an image can be seen, and thus the sensible motion of external objects is really no more than a series of images with gaps between. All of which means that we do not see continuity. The same is true of the other sense-impressions, as there is always a time-factor involved in any sensible recognition. Again, when we analyze motion we always give it a granular structure, even though our ultimate fixed elements are infinitesimals. Thus, both experience and thought deal with manifolds, and never with true continua. In this connection the analysis of Weierstrass is profoundly significant. By very careful thinking Weierstrass reached the conclusion that there is no such thing as motion, but only a series of different states or positions occupied by objects. As a judgment or interpretation concerning the universe of objects in its purity as abstracted from the whole, I do not see how this statement can be seriously questioned. It simply means that the ceaseless becoming and endless dying, which mark the universe of objects, are series of instantaneous states rather than true continua. This would be the rigorous interpretation of being as it appears to objective consciousness in isolation from other dimensions of consciousness, and thus radically nonmystical. It reveals beautifully the absence of depth or substance in the universe when taken in abstraction as only objective. The series of states are no more than dead pictures, having no life or substance, but are merely empty terms in relation.

The inverse of the phantasmagoric series, which constitutes the universe of experience and thought in its purity as abstracted, is the true continuum. The one is a granular manifold, the other a flowing unity. Now it is true that man has arrived at the notion of continuity, although, as Weierstrass has shown, he never really thinks it. Continuity is the inverse of the manifold and is, of necessity, recognized at the moment man became conscious of manifoldness, but this recognition involves more than the action of consciousness in the objective sense. Continuity belongs to the hinterland of consciousness. This simply illustrates the eternal fact, i.e., that the actual consciousness of man continually operates in a Nirvanic as well as in a Sangsaric sense. However, analysis has grappled fairly well with the Sangsaric phase, but has remained generally not-self-conscious with respect to the Nirvanic.

This all leads us to the point that the unity of the Nirvanic Consciousness is better symbolized by the notion of the true continuum than by the finite number 1 (one). For the number one is a fixed entity representing a single empty term, which in turn always implies the manifold of all numbers. In other words, the unity of numeral one is an abstraction and not a concrete actuality. It is the unity of the continuum, in the true sense, that symbolizes the unity of the Nirvanic State. The Nirvanic Consciousness is not granular but flowing. It is without parts, in the sense of finite proper parts, but is a ceaselessly flowing and self-contained stream. It is not a stream from past to the future, that implies division by the point called the "present," but a flowing that comprehends the totality that appears in the universe of objects as the temporal series.

That which appears in man as the persistent Self— the Witness of the universe-drama—is the dividing and uniting point of two worlds of consciousness. Before our consciousness lies the universe of objects, but behind is the hinterland of the Self, and this is Nirvana. But the hinterland of the Self is also the hinterland of all objects. In this hinterland we do not have merely empty terms in relation, perceived by the Self; we have a continuum in which the inverse of the self is identical with the inverse of all objects. Here consciousness, substance, and energy, or life, are interchangeable terms. Here, also, the sterile and empty terms-in-relation are replaced by a pregnant Meaning. Without this Meaning man simply cannot live. The more closely man identifies himself with objects, or mere empty terms-in-relation, the more starved he becomes, and in the end, if this condition is continued too far, real death must follow. By real death I mean the loss of self-consciousness.

Actually, man has rarely succeeded in *completely* isolating himself from the inflow of consciousness from the hinterland. For the greater part, he has simply received this inflow and has not succeeded in being self-conscious with respect to it. Unknowingly, he has received some nourishment, otherwise life in the universe of objects would have failed e'er now. Yet, except for a few among the human whole, the stream of nourishment has been so poor that man suffers the travail of slow starvation. Great is the need that the stream be increased. Now, this increase is accomplished by opening the gates to the hinterland through at least some degree of Recognition. This means becoming self-conscious, in at least some measure, of the stream of Nirvanic Consciousness and realizing oneself as identical with it. We need more philosophy conceived as a Way of Life and less emphasis upon systems of bare terms-in-relation.

It has been stated that the key to Nirvanic Consciousness consists of an anesthetizing of the power of experiencing and of thinking, combined with a continuing of self-consciousness. This is the essential process that reveals the significance of the step. Practically, the process of transformation may or may not involve the complete anesthetizing. If the anesthesia is complete, then the consciousness of the universe of objects is wholly annulled, either temporarily or permanently. This is the mystic destruction of the universe and the Awakening to the Nirvanic State. Objectively viewed, the individual who does this appears to enter a complete state of ecstatic trance, in which there is a suspension of vital and conscious process in the Sangsaric sense. This is all that the physical scientist qua physical scientist can observe. And if the observer holds to the theory that the Sangsaric type of consciousness is the only possible consciousness, then he would say the trance involved the total extinction of consciousness in every sense. Some psychologists take this position, but since they are unable to trace what they cannot see, they are quite unqualified to pass judgment upon the state in question. For in this matter the bare observer is entirely helpless. The realizer may report the continuity of his self-consciousness, but the observer, as such, has no check whatsoever. If, in turn, he should become a realizer in his own right, then he would Know, but that knowing would not be the result of his observing external states or conditions. He would no longer be a bare observer.

Now, it is possible, by a modified technique, to become a realizer and remain, in some degree, an observer at the same time. In this case, there is substituted for the literal anesthetizing a process of dissociation of the two kinds of consciousness. The thinking and experiencing powers are set on one side, as it were, while the larger portion of the self-conscious principle, but not all, is withdrawn into the hinterland. In this case, there is no black-out trance-state but a sort of slowing down of the Sangsaric consciousness and the objective life-stream. It is a critical kind of balance to maintain, as there is a constant tendency for the consciousness principle to "flop over" completely to the one side or the other. But if, through steadiness of the will, the balance is maintained and the self-analyzing power functions with clear discrimination, then it is possible to be conscious on two levels without confusion. In this case, dissociation accomplishes the essential effect of the anesthesia.

The latter technique has a decided advantage in that it effects a conscious bridging of two levels of consciousness. This facilitates the construction of interpretative symbols, and as well, opens a door whereby a stream of Nirvanic Consciousness may be made to penetrate the universe of objects and be more or less consciously directed.

From the standpoint of Consciousness-without-an-object there is no problem concerning immortality. The directly known truth is: "Immortality is, but no embodied or object-bound stage of consciousness is immortal." This simply means that the Sea of Consciousness is without beginning or end, being completely unconditioned by time, but the various stages wherein that Sea supports objects are temporary. Thus man as man is not immortal. Here it must be understood that 'man', as well as any other name of an object, is only a designation for a stage along the Way. Immortality attaches to consciousness as a principle, not to the stages. Man may achieve immortality by superimposing his evolved power of self-consciousness upon the Primordial Consciousness itself, but in this case he simply ceases to be a man. The self-conscious Nirvani is no longer a man, though in his case the differentiated consciousness-principle once passed through the human stage. Actually, the Nirvani is a Divine, rather than a human, being. The consciousness-principle is the Pilgrim that passes through many stages, absorbing from those stages many values in terms of progressively awakened self-consciousness. When man succeeds in assimilating the Pilgrim by transference of his self-consciousness, then his self-identity is one with immortal consciousness, but the self-identity ceases to be merely human. Put in other terms, all somatic stages are temporary; the consciousness stream is without beginning or end.

But while immortality ceases to be a problem, an entirely different problem arises. This may be stated in the form: How is it possible, within a beginningless and endless Primordial Consciousness, for transitory states to arise? I am not here attempting any solution of this problem but simply indicating the shift of problem form. This new problem, unlike the old one concerning immortality, has no tragic implications. Reflective consciousness, aided by insight and observation, may undertake its resolution at leisure, with all the time in the world to complete the search. For with the problem thus stated, there is no deep religious or psychological need at stake. The resolution of the problem would have theoretical and working value, but there is no time-pressure to drive reflective consciousness to a quick solution.

There is but one consideration that I shall suggest here. It is unthinkable that the formless and attributeless Primordial Consciousness, all of a sudden, at a certain point, started to project Itself into the subject-object series of states. Rather, no beginning or end to the series of states is thinkable, one state being always the consequent of a preceding state and the cause of the one that follows. Consciousness-without-an-object is not a First Cause; it is the substratum underlying all possible states and causes.

For one who has made himself familiar with the stream of western philosophy from the time of the Greeks to the present day, it should be evident that there are certain differences of base and valuation that have divided philosophers throughout the whole of that period. The development of scientific knowledge, of mathematics, and of epistemological criticism has not succeeded in bridging these differences so that a philosophic agreement could be effected. All these developments have only had the effect of changing the form in which the differences appear, so that they have become more subtle and intellectually sophisticated; but the essential differences still remain, however much transformed in their statement. There still are incompatible philosophic schools, represented by men of comparable degrees of intellectual ability, training, and knowledge. All of which reveals, clearly, that the factors that make for philosophic differences run deeper than the material with which science can deal and resolve factually and interpretatively once for all.

Some psychologists have taken cognizance of these philosophical tendencies and have shown that they are connected with differences of psychological type. The immediately taken base and the accepted values are not the same for all men. And this immediate element belongs more to religion, in the broad and fundamental sense, than it does to science. It is something that precedes, rather than follows, science. In fact, that attitude that makes the scientific point of view itself possible is of the nature of these more fundamental and extrascientific adjustments. Justice demands that we accept these differences of adjustment as relatively valid and renounce the hope and desire for universal philosophic conformity. The conflict of philosophic schools is both desirable and necessary.

Two important types of differences in valuation and immediate insight will account for the principle differences of philosophic systems. One is a difference in the valuation of the two principal groups of objects, i.e., objects of sense and objects of thought. The other is a difference in the valuation of objectivity, as such, as contrasted to the subjective pole of consciousness. These differences I shall discuss briefly, so as to relate my own system to them more clearly.

Evidently the overwhelming majority of men in thought and practice most of the time predicate substantial reality of the objects of sensation, particularly in terms of the social waking consciousness of our ordinary life. Most, though not all, physical scientists take this position, as well as the majority of the men of action. Among the current philosophical tendencies

Naturalism definitely, and sometimes quite naively, takes this standpoint. This is also true in considerable degree, but not entirely, of the representatives of Pragmatism. The position of Neorealism is more involved, in that, while it is highly objective, its objects are not conceived as objects of sensation or of thought, but as independent existences that, in their real nature, are neither psychical nor physical, though capable of passing through both psychical and physical systems without being altered in their essential nature. However, Neorealism is frankly and intensely objective in its valuation, and therefore stands in closer relationship to both Pragmatism and Naturalism than it does to Idealism.

There is a smaller class of men who find the objects of thought more real than the objects of sensation. These are represented in the philosophical systems of rational Scholasticism, Rationalism proper, and in those philosophical systems currently called intellectualistic. There may be more or less blending between these philosophic currents and Naturalism, Neorealism, and Idealism, though they are definitely non-pragmatic, since the latter school seems pretty thoroughly united on the principle of anti-intellectualism, in the philosophic sense.

The two foregoing groups largely agree in that they attach primary importance to objects, in some sense, and may be divided by regarding one group as sensationalistic and the other as rationalistic or intellectualistic.

In contrast to both these groups there stand those who attach the greater reality to the subjective pole of consciousness. In the philosophies these are represented by Idealism and Vedantism. However, this class seems to be more widely represented by individuals whose dominant expression is not consciously philosophical.

More often their expression appears in the form of a mysticism that is more poetic than philosophical. Yet, within the mystical group, there is a further differentiation to be made between those who emphasize union with God and those who emphasize union with the Self in a transcendental sense. However, the whole mystical movement is in a subjective direction, so, when the emphasis is placed upon more or less Divine objects, these objects are subtle rather than gross.

In the present system all objects are regarded as derivative, and therefore possessing, at best, only a derivative or symbolic reality. Yet some objects may have a higher order of relative reality than others. I have already pointed out that the valuation here is relative to purpose and not absolute. Thus, the ordinary gross objects of sense, common to waking consciousness, are given no superior status as such. Essentially, dream objects and mystical objects are given the same validity. Relative to a particular purpose, the one or the other class of objects may be judged as possessing the superior order of reality. Concerning the two classes of objects, i.e., objects of sensation whether subtle or gross, and objects of thought, the same principle applies. Objects of thought, or some classes of the objects of thought, may, in some purposive situations, possess an inferior reality as compared to that attaching to the objects of sensation. On the other hand, the reverse is equally true in other purposive situations. To sum up: All objects of whatever type, whether objects for sensation or for thought, whether subtle or gross, whether abstract or concrete, in the last analysis possess only a derivative reality, and thus may be regarded finally as a *seeming* only.

There remains to be considered the view this system presents concerning the subjective pole of consciousness. In this, I am referring to that which is variously known as the 'ego', whether in the personal or higher sense, the 'I', the 'self', or the 'Atman', whether in the individual or supreme sense. In this subjective pole there are discernible differentia, just as there are between different classes of objects. Now, in the present system, the subjective pole, both in its inferior and superior aspects, is viewed as the reflex or inverse of the object, as such, though in the higher sense it is viewed as essentially the higher pole. This means that the 'I', in whatever sense, whether empiric or transcendental, is as much derivative as the objective world. Thus the present system is not to be identified with either Vedantism or current Idealism, though it is arrived at by a process of passing through these schools of interpretation and thus stands genetically, although not necessarily formally, closer to them.

The final position is: The One, nonderivative Reality, is THAT which I have symbolized by "Consciousness-without-an-object." This is Root Consciousness, per se, to be distinguished from consciousness as content or as state, on the one hand, and from consciousness as an attribute of a Self or Atman, in any sense whatsoever. It is Consciousness of which nothing can be predicated in the privative sense save abstract Being. Upon It all else depends, while It remains self-existent.

The question of the means by which any individual may arrive at a direct Realization of Consciousness-without-an-object is one that is very involved and the solution has many variants, corresponding to the psychical status of the various individuals. All evidence confirms the view that it is reached by a progressive series of steps, such that a lower attachment or identification is renounced for one that is superior, the process being repeated again and again until, from the vantage ground of a high transcendental position, the final step can be taken. Beyond this general statement the question of technique cannot be entered into here.

Apart from the actual Realization of Consciousness-without-an-object, it is possible to take the symbol itself as an object of thought and use it for the purpose of philosophical and general mystical integration. This is the procedure of assuming the symbol as a fundamental premise and then observing the consequences that follow. There is some reason to believe that such a method of procedure is possible within the setting of western culture, as might not be the case for oriental culture or for any culture that has preceded ours of which any record exists. This possibility I see as growing out of our peculiar mathematical development. In mathematics we excel all other cultures, and as I see it, all other genuine superiority we may have has resulted from this mathematical excellence. In other respects, as far as the greater and durable values are concerned, there are other cultures in the Orient, whether of the present or the past, that just as clearly excel ours. Now, it is by its power, and not its weakness, that an individual or a class attains the best. Thus, I would select the mathematical road as the one of preeminent power so far as western culture is concerned.

Now the validity of mathematics is established upon a basis that is quite impersonal and universal. Its authority is not dependent upon the name of any writer of any mathematical treatise. In its purity it deals only with the transcendental or ideal objects of the very highest order of thinkable abstraction or universality. In high degree, the consciousness of the mathematician qua mathematician is not concerned with either a self or objects. To be sure, this is not absolutely so, but this position is attained in mathematical consciousness in higher degree than anywhere else, except in states of Samadhi of a high order. Herein is revealed the power of pure mathematics as an instrument of consciousness-transformation on a very lofty level.

Again, pure mathematics is the only real invariant that we have in the ever-changing phantasmagoria of experience. When an individual undertakes to chart an unknown sea, he must have fixed bases of reference by which to navigate his course, if he would not run the risk of being hopelessly lost. To be sure, there is a profound sense in which the pure Self is a similar invariant, but the peculiar psychology of the West is too objective in its orientation to permit this Self to be generally and effectively accessible. It is otherwise in India. This profound psychological difference renders it impractical to hope to graft oriental method upon the western man, save in some exceptional cases. That would be using the right method with the wrong man, and such a procedure leads to wrong results. Hence, the western psychology being what it is, the available invariant seems to be pure mathematics.

I am not speaking with a naive ignorance of current philosophic and logical analysis of pure mathematics. But I shall not enter into this extremely technical question at this time. I am well aware that the invariant element does not lie in the fundamental assumptions, or so-called axioms, from which a mathematical system starts. These assumptions may be chosen as a largely free creative act, but just as soon as the process of deduction of theorems begins, free creativeness ceases. The law that governs the flow of consequences is tougher than tempered steel and harder than the hardest rock. Save in the Self, here, as nowhere else, is there something to which human consciousness can tie and give its trust, though all else became fluid and confusing. And this invulnerable core carries straight through to Consciousness-without-an-object. Only at the very last does the logical invariant vanish in the eternally Ineffable, but then the Wanderer has arrived at the place of Final Security and Completeness, beyond the relativity of all science, art, religion, and philosophy.

And supposing the Wanderer has at last arrived, is there nothing more than a ceaseless consciousness without content? No, before him there stand all possibilities, both those of the universe of objects, in every sense, and also of Nirvana, likewise in every sense. But the arrived Wanderer is now Enlightened and is secure against all dangers and all possible entanglements in all kingdoms or states of consciousness from the heavens to the Hells. He may produce creatively or not, but in any case He is superior to either action or refraining from action. In a word, He moves upon the plane of a higher order of evolution. This is the meaning of Consciousness-without-an-object.

Notes to Chapter 5

1. It would be more correct to say that the older conception can no longer interpret the facts as *simply* as the newer conception. It is always possible to make the older conception work by adding intricate interpretations through *ad hoc* hypotheses, but this is done at the price of clumsiness and complication. It is not change in the factual picture that compels change in theory, but the greater logical beauty and efficacy of the new theory.

2. According to latest theory, the radiation density at the early, highly condensed stage of the expanding universe was much higher than the matter density. What matter there was present was, however, spread out uniformly. At a later stage of expansion the radiation density had dropped to equality with that of matter, and at this point "gravitational instability" set in and the galaxies began forming.

3. Actually, the more generally valid space-time "invariant" concept is that of the directed quantity "Energy-Momentum," of which "Energy" is merely that part lying along the direction of increasing time. For the sake of simplicity of illustration we use only the more familiar term "Energy."

4. This analogue is not employed to suggest that the aphorisms gain their authority from the physical conception. Physical conceptions change and so constructions based upon them are vulnerable. The real point made is that the aphorisms, as concepts, are not nearly as strange as they may seem at first. The above is a conceptual pattern that already exists and is used, though in a somewhat different sector of human knowledge. Of necessity, any conceptual symbol must be composed in terms of the conceptualism of its milieu, however unthinkable its roots may be in conceptual terms.

5. In this connection, by fundamental theory I mean one that is a primary assumption of a given type of intellect— its starting point for creative constructions. These fundamental theories are based in faith and really form part of the essential religious belief of a given culture. In order to think, we must always start with something that we cannot prove either by logic or by reference to experience. This something defines the form of experience as it becomes the material of thought, but it is not a derivative from experience. Thus, for example, our science rests upon a faith in the uniformity of nature. Discredit this faith and the science falls as a whole. Indeed, this faith may be perfectly justified, but it precedes science—it does not follow from science. In psychologic terms, the fundamental theory wells out of the unconscious.

6. This is perhaps the most concrete special case of the energy-momentum concept described in a previous note.

7. An implication of the foregoing discussion is that physical science does not give us noumenal, metaphysical, or substantive knowledge. Rather it gives an only positivistic kind of knowledge, but a positivism that is logical as well as aesthetic.

8. The following questions have been raised: "What is the interpretation of an 'individual center of consciousness'?" "Is it a void too?" First, with respect to the individual center of consciousness, it may be said that we mean here the empiric

cognizing entities that we commonly view as individuals, without raising at this point the question as to the ultimate status of individuality. But the second question raises problems having profound ramifications which are given serious consideration in a future volume. The whole issue between the Atma Vidya of the Vedantins and the Anatmic doctrine of the Buddhists is raised in this question. Briefly, it may be stated that the position taken here occupies an intermediate position. Thus it would be said that in the relative sense the individual center of consciousness is not a void or unreal as compared with the object, but in the absolute sense it may be viewed as a void in the sense of being ultimately derivative. It occupies a position analogous to that of the concept of the parameter as used in mathematics.

9. The older psychology without a psyche is merely a crude physical science.

10. The assurance of the transcendental states is by no means a certainty that the conceptual interpretation is the most correct possible. Interpretation is a relative function subject to criticism.

Chapter 6

COMMENTARIES ON THE APHORISMS

●

PRELIMINARY

In their depths, feeling and thought spring from the same root. This root, in its own nature as unmanifested, has a character that appears to the relative consciousness as both devoid of feeling and without conceptual form. But when realized, it has the value of fulfilled feeling and completed thought. Consciousness no longer feels a reaching out for an unattained completeness. With this, both thought and feeling lose their differentiated and, therefore, identifiable particularity. But when the root is projected into the actualizing consciousness, it loses some measure of its purity, since to actualize is to particularize, even though on the most abstract level of expression. The aphorisms on Consciousness-without-an-object constitute such a projection on a level of exceptional abstraction and universality, whereby the unthinkable becomes, in some measure, the thinkable. But since, in this act, the universal comprehender appears in the field of the comprehended, we stand, in the latter case, not in the presence of Truth herself, but we come into possession of a symbol of the Truth.

To step from the symbol to that which is symbolized, though this does afford a peculiarly exacting demand upon acuity of thought, yet requires much more. Here, feeling, in the best sense, must fuse with the thought. Thus the thinker must learn also to feel his thought, so that, in the highest degree, he thinks devotedly. It is not enough to think clearly, if the thinker stands aloof, not giving *himself* with his thought. The thinker arrives by surrendering himself to Truth, claiming for himself no rights save those that Truth herself bestows upon him. In the final state of perfection he possesses no longer opinions of his own nor any private preference. Then Truth possesses him, not he, Truth.

He who would become one with the Eternal must first learn to be humble. He must offer, upon the sacrificial altar, the pride of the knower. He must become one who lays no possessive claim to knowledge or wisdom. This is the state of the mystic ignorance— of the emptied heart. He who has thus become as nothing in his own right then is prepared to become possessed by Wisdom herself. The completeness of self-emptying is the precondition to the realization of unutterable Fullness. Thus mere "knowledge about" becomes transformed into Knowledge as Reality.

To know THAT which the aphorisms symbolize is to be possessed by THAT and, then, to be one with THAT. Thenceforth, all thinking, all feeling, all particularization, and all selfhood lie below. To be sure, all these remain, but no longer as claimants to a Throne they could not possibly fill. They remain thenceforth as the actors in the Divine Drama, but no more.

Before the candidate the ordeal of the mystic death appears as a terror-inspiring apparition. But he who, with stout heart challenging the seeming of ultimate dissolution, enters into the awful and terrible presence, finds only utter Glory. Terror has become beatitude. Only liabilities have been lost as he finds himself, not lost in the Eternal, but become that Eternal Itself. All the dangers of the Way are only ghosts, possessing no power save such as the candidate has himself projected upon them. However, since there is much darkness and fear in the heart of man, there are apparitions of terrible visage. But they have no power of their own and must vanish, helpless before the will of the undaunted candidate.

He who receives the aphorisms as guideposts along the Way will find in them powers to dissipate all apparitions, whether of terror or seduction. The threatening appearance of darkness will be dissipated before him as he journeys along his Path. In the end, the Door to Glory will loom clear before his gaze, and he will know no conflict with terror in any part of the Way. Yet he who does not find himself able to go so far, may yet find in the symbols content for his thought that will illumine that thought. Thought in the light is much better than thought groping in darkness. To think from the base of Light, though it be that that Light is not yet understood, is far better than thought grounded in the darkness of no vision. For upon some base all thought must be grounded if it is to be more than that absolute nescience that leads in darkness from nowhere to nowhere. To have more than such hopeless darkness, he, who is not yet Knowledge, must base himself upon faith, whether it be faith in the Eternal, or some lesser light. Lacking Knowledge, man must have faith if he would not perish.

1 . . . Consciousness-without-an-object is.

The fundamental principle underlying all the aphorisms is that Consciousness is the original and self-existent Reality. This Consciousness is both Substance and Life. It would be possible to view the Primordial Principle in terms of Life or of Substance, as well as in terms of Consciousness, but I approach the subject from the standpoint of Consciousness for the reason that this is the phase of Reality of which we are most immediately certain. Consciousness, Life, and Substance are not to be regarded as three distinct realities, but as merely three facets of the nondual Reality, as the latter appears to the analytic consciousness.

The Primordial Consciousness is not to be regarded as the consciousness of some transcendent being who is aware of some content. Herein lies, perhaps, the main difficulty with respect to understanding the idea contained in the symbol of Consciousness-without-an-object. We are in the habit of regarding consciousness as something derivative—a quality possessed by something else or a kind of relationship. It is necessary to abandon this view if the aphorisms are to be understood. Let this Consciousness be considered as original, and then both the subject and object become derivative. That which is primary and original, then, is a Great Void of Consciousness, to all consciousness of the type that depends upon the subject-object relationship. It is as though that Consciousness were nothing, while actually It is the all in all.

This Absolute Consciousness is, from the relative standpoint, indistinguishable from unconsciousness. Most generally, philosophy is written from the perspective that views the ultimate as unconscious, whether of psychical (e.g., von Hartmann's view) or non-psychical (e.g., the view of materialists) nature, and thus has taken the relative consciousness as the ground of approach, but the aphorisms are written as from the ultimate Transcendental Base, and then, from that viewpoint the problems of relative consciousness are approached. We are following a deductive process of descent from the most universal to the concrete or particular, rather than the inductive method that is so characteristic of physical science and much philosophy, including that of von Hartmann.

An inevitable question is: How can this Primordial Consciousness be known? To this it is answered, "Through a Recognition transcending the Nirvanic State." Complete verification of the validity of the aphorisms requires this. However, a partial or pragmatic verification may be achieved through willing to accept them *as though* they were true symbols of the Reality, and then drawing the consequences that follow from them, finally noting how they affect the problems of life and thought as practically experienced. If the investigator finds that they tend to simplify the problems and to bring the self into more harmonious adjustment with the not-self, then they prove to be an orientation that enriches life, and are thus pragmatically justified.

Naturally, it is implied that Recognition is a human possibility. Otherwise, the aphorisms would have to rest upon one or the other of two bases: (*a*) intellectual speculation grounded exclusively in relative consciousness; or (*b*) external superhuman revelation beyond the possibility of human verification. Both these standpoints are denied here, especially the latter. The notion of external superhuman revelation, when subjected to analysis, does not possess any really intelligible meaning, and belief in this tends toward both intellectual and moral suicide. From this belief follows the attitude made famous in the words of Tertullian: "I believe because it is against reason." Such a viewpoint is utterly foreign to the spirit in which the aphorisms are written.

It is affirmed that the aphorisms mean a content given through immediate Knowledge, and that for the Realization of this content the functioning of a generally latent organ is the proximate means. Hence they are not to be viewed as metaphysical speculations of which the concepts would have no real content, as Kant pointed out in his *Critique of Pure Reason* in relation to metaphysical subject-matter. Thus it is maintained that the aphorisms are not mere developments of the pure reason, and accordingly, avoid the challenge of the Kantian criticism. Therefore, philosophic criticism of the present philosophy, in so far as it is strictly philosophical, must assume the actuality of the inner organ.

The critical problem takes the form: Does the inner organ or Samadhindriya—as it is known in Sanscrit—exist? This is a psychological, or rather, metapsychological question. I have explored with care the possibilities of logical proof that such an organ must exist, but have been forced to conclude that no such demonstration is possible. Yet logical disproof is equally impossible. The only possible proof depends upon immediate experience of the activity of the organ. On the other hand, empiric disproof is impossible, since empiric disproof of any supposed psychical function or organ presupposes demonstrably complete knowledge of every psychical possibility. I am not aware that any psychologist lays claim to such omniscience.

Now, if any individual should have immediate acquaintance with the functioning of a psychical organ, which with most men either lies wholly inactive or functions in such a way as to be unrecognizable to the relative consciousness of the individual, he would know as a matter of genuine private knowledge that the function or organ is an actuality. But if he sought to prove this actuality to those in whom the function was wholly latent, he would face serious difficulties. Anything that he succeeded in introducing into the consciousness of the latter would, of necessity, be in terms of the functions that were already active in them. In general, this means in terms of the so-called five-sense rational consciousness. Anything more that was strictly peculiar to the new organ would stand in incommensurable relationship, and therefore, be ineffable; it could not be communicated at all. But that which could be communicated would be, as said, in terms of the usual five-sense rational content. And this could always be explained away by the appropriate ingenuity, so that it would appear to the unawakened consciousness that the hypothesis of a new organ was unnecessary. The inventive ingenuity of the human intellect is, undoubtedly, quite capable of inventing the appropriate hypotheses. But if, for instance, the born-blind could invent hypotheses that would explain everything that the seeing ones could convey to their consciousness, in terms that could dispense with the hypothesis that anybody had sight, this might be quite convincing to other blind men, but it would leave those who had sight quite unimpressed. The result would be a stalemate.

That the conception of a latent mystical sense, active in some instances but inactive with most men, can be interpreted in such a way as to supply a *sufficient* explanation of how a transcendental knowledge can be, I have not yet found questioned by anyone. It is the question of *necessity* that is raised. Now, if we assume the actuality of the mystical sense in an active state in a given case, then, although the content that could be conveyed into the zone of the ordinary five-sense rational consciousness would not necessarily require the predication of the mystical sense for its interpretation, yet there would remain the incommensurable or ineffable portion of the original content or state, which still would require explanation. So far as I have found, the hypotheses of the five-sense rational consciousness imply that the ineffable content or value is pure illusion. To the mystic this is proof of the *insufficiency* of all such hypotheses, since he claims a greater reality-quale for the content or value realized through the mystical sense than for that possessed by all the other senses. Now, how is the five-sense rational consciousness going to challenge this? By basic assumption the mystic has the five-sense rational consciousness plus all the consciousness-value realized through the mystic sense, and therefore, is in a position to establish a comparative valuation; and this the exclusively five-sense rational consciousness cannot do. At this point the less gentlemanly of the psychologists descend to the street urchin's device of labeling the other fellow with bad names, though usually highly technical language is employed. I submit that this is beneath the dignity of true scholars and gentlemen.

It is a principle of logic that a rigorous argument shall satisfy the categories of both necessity and sufficiency. But this perfection is attained only in pure mathematics. No inductive, hence no scientific, hypothesis satisfies both these conditions. There is no scientific hypothesis that is necessary in the logical sense, since other hypotheses could be invented. But a scientific hypothesis must pass the test of sufficiency, i.e., it must be such as to incorporate *all* relevant facts into a systematic whole. Now, if we are to leave out mutual name-calling as a valid line of argument as between the possessors of the mystic sense and those of the exclusive five-sense type, then it is the five-sense type of interpretative theory that fails to satisfy the canons of scientific hypotheses. For these hypotheses do not satisfy the condition of sufficiency.

As to the ineffable content or quality of mystical states of consciousness, it may be pointed out that there is nothing at all strange about this. "Ineffable" means unspeakable or incommunicable. But incommunicability is not at all strange, for such a limitation attaches even to sense-experience. The peculiar quale of one sense cannot be communicated in terms that are understandable with respect to another sense. And indeed, there is something fundamentally ineffable in the relationship between percepts and concepts. Concepts convey perceptual values from one individual to another only to the extent that the two individuals have a commonality of perceptual experience. Since the referents are in common the concepts convey meaning, but otherwise they do not. Now, the mystic knows an ineffable content or quality *in the case of communication to a nonmystic,* but in general, the concept, the sign, or symbol will convey this content, more or less adequately, to a fellow mystic. It is just a case of the concepts, signs, or symbols having a different kind of reference and of two or more individuals having common acquaintance with the relevant referents.

In the highest sense of Transcendental Consciousness we have to abandon the whole idea of organ of consciousness, since the notion of organ implies delimitation. But so long as there are stages in mystical consciousness, the idea of an inner organ is valid.

2 . . . Before objects were, Consciousness-without-an-object is.

This aphorism emphasizes the priority of Consciousness to content. But this is not a priority in time in the sense that a causal antecedent precedes a consequent. Primordial Consciousness is no more a cause of objects, *in the temporal sense*, than is space a cause of the stellar systems. But without space there could be no stellar systems, and likewise, there could be no objects without the support of Consciousness. Hence Consciousness-without-an-object is, not in the sense of a present that is a mere point in the flow of the future into the past, but in the sense of an Eternal Now. This "isness" is a denial of time. Consciousness-without-an-object is not a cause that determines any particularization, but it is the Causeless-Cause whereby all particularization is possible.

Here "Objects" must be understood in that most general sense of any modification of consciousness whatsoever. It is not only objects as seen or thought, but, as well, any feeling-toned state of consciousness. For, a feeling-toned state, being recognizable as such, is, therefore, a content or object.

We cannot conceive of a first object, since before that object there must be its causal antecedent. The stream of objects is a stream reaching from nowhere in the past to nowhere in the future. There is no substance in this time-stream, and hence an eon of eons is precisely the same as the smallest division of time, just as a finite section in a line is as rich in points as the infinite totality of the line. The drama of time is played in the Sea of Consciousness, and yet it is as though nothing at all had happened.

3 . . . Though objects seem to exist,
Consciousness-without-an-object is.

This aphorism relates to that state wherein objects, in any sense, appear to consciousness *now*, whereas the preceding aphorism refers to that which seems to be before the present appearance. All existence that objects may have is for the "now" only, though we may distinguish phases of the "now," such as existence in memory, existence as given in the present presentation, and existence in the imagination as future. There is a recognizable qualitative difference between these three phases of the "now," but no phase can be actually isolated from the "now" of consciousness and still have existence, in any sense, predicated of it. For predication is a present act within consciousness itself.

In the first part of this aphorism, the crucial word is "seem." No object requires more than *seeming* in order to exist for consciousness. Existence conceived in any other sense, than as for consciousness, is entirely meaningless. For that existence is found to be dependent upon *being conceived*, which, of necessity, is a conscious act or state. In the strictest logical sense, therefore, all objects rest upon the same base, i.e., that of *seeming*. To be sure, purposive interest will lead to the abstraction of certain objects as being important, while others will remain in greater or less degree irrelevant. Relative to purpose, then, degrees of reality or unreality may be predicated of the manifold of all objects. But this predication is valid only in relation to the given purpose, and confusion arises when this is forgotten. Thus, for some purposes, the dream-object may be more real than the objects of our so-called waking consciousness. For the purposes of our scientific culture, a certain class of objects belonging to the waking state is significant. We have formed the habit of calling these real, and of thinking of them as being real in some nonrelative sense. In this we forget that the reality that they possess is relative only to our specific scientific purpose. Our psychologists tend to distinguish between this class of objects and all, or nearly all, other objects by calling the latter phantasy. This is a terminology that is prejudicial to the latter class and is not logically justified, unless the condition is explictly implied that they are phantastic and unreal with respect to a certain scientific interest. Considered *as such*, apart from any purposive motive, we cannot distinguish any relative difference in degree or reality as attaching to any class of objects when contrasted to other objects. All objects are equal in that their existence is a *seeming* to consciousness and no more. But whether there is one kind of purpose or another, or a complete absence of all purpose, consciousness, per se, is an indisputable reality. This Consciousness is a Reality that unites, on the one hand, the youngest child, the idiot, or the insane, with the wisest and most developed intelligence, on the other. The differences that mark the gulf between these extremes are differences in content only, and not of Consciousness taken apart from content.

There is no doubt but that a valid significance attaches to difference in valuation of the various contents of consciousness. But these valuations are always relative to purpose and level, and not significant out of relation to all purpose or perspective. Thus valuation, itself, is but one of the derivative contents of consciousness, subject to development and decay. Beneath valuation, as the substratum that makes it, as well as all else, possible, is pure Consciousness apart from content.

> 4 . . . When objects vanish,
> yet remaining through all unaffected,
> Consciousness-without-an-object is.

Objects have vanished when they are no longer present to consciousness as currently present, or present in memory, or finally, present in imagination. The fact of vanishing is not affected by the arising of other objects. Thus, vanishing operates as a principle, whether it is complete or only partial.

Consciousness-without-an-object is the binding principle underlying the progression and evanescence of states or objects of consciousness. This binding principle neither develops nor disintegrates. It is thus the invariant element associated with all variation. At certain stages in the analysis of consciousness it appears as though the invariant element were the pure Subject or the Self, but at this stage the analysis has not isolated the subtle distinction between pure Subjectivity and Consciousness, as such. It thus appears as though the pure Self were a sort of permanent atomic nucleus, which is persistent through all states. But, when analysis is carried further, this notion is seen to fail. Ultimately, it is found that the Self is derivative as well as the objective pole of consciousness. Thus, there remains as the sole nonderivative principle the Pure Consciousness Itself.[1]

Just as we must regard the presence of objects as a seeming, and no more, so is the vanishing only a seeming. The nonderivative Reality is unaffected in either case.

5 . . . Outside of Consciousness-without-an-object nothing is.

Within the widely current realistic and naturalistic thought, both naive and critical, there is a deeply imbedded habit of viewing objects as existing quite independently of consciousness. From this perspective, objects are viewed as self-existent things. But this is a hypothetical construction, in the invidious sense, for the simple reason that it is incapable of verification, either through experience or as a necessity of thought. For verification necessarily implies the presence of consciousness, and so the, so-called, independent thing is reduced to the status of an object in dependent relationship to consciousness, at the moment of verification. There is no necessity, such as a logical necessity, that requires the predication of the existence of things quite independent of consciousness, in every sense, in order to account for the arising of objects. For objects arise and vanish with respect to a *state* of consciousness, and merely cease to be traceable beyond the borders of that state, for that state alone. Their continued existence for another state beyond those borders is not only in principle possible, but is verifiable through the use of the appropriate means. Though logic and the principle of causal connection may require that the arising of objects shall not be completely *de novo*, it is not necessary to predicate existence of things, totally independent of consciousness, in order to satisfy this requirement.

Objects, for the state of waking consciousness, vanish upon going to sleep, and an entirely different state or system of objects is realized. But though the system of objects that may be realized in the dream state is quite different, the analysis of dreams has often shown a connection between some of these objects and the contents of the waking state. Some dreams reveal a continuity of objects from past waking states, while others are prophetic with respect to objects experienced in future waking states. Here we have an instance of a widely experienced movement of consciousness from state to state with objects traceable in quite different systems of objects. These two examples of specific states, admittedly, are insufficient to trace the whole genetic and disintegrative history of objects. But they do afford empiric demonstration of the possibility of consciousness to shift from state to state, and thus render conceivable, in principle, the broader application of this possibility. Thus, again, there is no logical or epistemological need to predicate the existence of things apart from consciousness.

The aphorism goes further than barely to affirm that the predication of the existence of things, outside consciousness in every sense, is unnecessary. It asserts, categorically that "Outside of Consciousness-without-an-object nothing is." This may be viewed as simply implying a primary definition of "something." Thus "something" is that which is an object in consciousness in some sense. Actually, no meaning attaches to the notion of "something" in any other sense. Such a notion is useless, as well as unnecessary. To say "outside of consciousness in every sense there exists thus and so" is just to produce a meaningless collection of words, like the classical combination, "the barren woman's son."

6 . . . Within the bosom of
Consciousness-without-an-object lies
the power of awareness that projects objects.

Pure Primordial Consciousness must be conceived as enveloping the subjective power of awareness, in relation to which objects exist. The subjective power of awareness and the content of consciousness stand in a relation of interdependence. In the most abstract case, wherein there is a consciousness of absence of objects, this absence has the value of content, since it stands in polar relationship to the subjective power of awareness. Thus there is no subject for which there is no content, in every sense, or stated conversely, where there is no content, there is no subjective pole of awareness.

Consciousness-without-an-object is not simply the power of awareness, for It comprehends the content along with the power of awareness itself. The power of awareness we may conceive as the first modification of the unmodified. It has its roots in, and derives its being from, the unmodified. It is this power that may be regarded as the First Cause—a Power that is Ever-Concealed, but renders possible the revealed and re-flected.

Ordinarily we think of the power of awareness as playing a purely passive or receptive role in the receiving of impressions. It is true that on the empiric level it does function, in some measure, in the receptive sense. But in the ordinary creative activity of men, even, we can see that this is not its exclusive function. Thus, a work of art is first creatively imagined, then projected into objective form, and finally, received back as an impression. In turn, the received impression may arouse further creative activity and lead to a repetition of the same process. However, in this series, the function of the received impression is that of a catalytic agent, which simply arouses the creatively projective power. It is the impression from the object that is passive and not the power of awareness. Clarity with respect to this point is of the very highest importance, as it is right here that the invidious participation in objects begins. When an individual views the power of awareness as standing in passive relationship to impressions from objects, he places himself in a position of subordination to objects, and this constitutes the essence of bondage. The universe of objects then becomes a great prison-house, instead of the playground of free creative activity. As a prison-house, the universe of objects takes on the seeming of evil—the great adversary of man—but as the playground of free creative activity, it is an invaluable agent for the progressive arousal of self-consciousness.

The projective power of awareness is a priori, i.e., it precedes experience. It is true that experience, in turn, reacts upon this power, but it acts as a stimulating, rather than as an essential, agent. The whole externally causal series consists only of such stimulating agents. While the stimulating agent may be viewed as a sort of trigger cause of subsequent creative projection, it is not the material cause. The *purely* creative phase of the projective power is a first cause from which effects follow, but that is not itself an effect of previous causes. At this point energy flows into the universe of objects. It is a misconception that an equation may be set up between any two states of the universe of objects, as between any two such states there may be an actual increase or decrease of content. The creative projection effects an increase of content.

7 . . . *When objects are projected,*
the power of awareness as subject is presupposed,
yet Consciousness-without-an-object
remains unchanged.

The projected objects become the experienced objects, and the latter appear to be a restricting environment. The restriction is a constant irritation, and thus is the basis of the ubiquitous suffering that runs through the worlds of objective experience. The ultimate effect of this irritation is to arouse the latent power of consciousness to be conscious of itself, an effect that could not be developed where there is no seeming of restriction placed upon the free play of consciousness. Out of consciousness of the consciousness of objects there is finally aroused the inverse realization of the subjective principle. We thus find the substratum on which all objects rest. By superimposing an objective character upon this substratum, we evolve the notion of an ego having an atomic existence analogous to that of objects, save that we give to it a fixed character in contradistinction to the ever-changing character of all genuine objects. The ego is thus produced as a compound of the atomic nature of objects and the relatively deathless persistence of pure subjectivity. But this atomic ego is a false construction, and not the genuine subjectivity. It is, in fact, but another object in the universe of objects; however, it is the peculiarly invidious object whereby consciousness is especially bound.

The true Recognition of the pure Subject is something quite different, in that the Self must be so recognized as never to become a new subtle object. It is that which underlies all notions, but is never itself a notion.

The aphorism reasserts the immutability of Consciousness-without-an-object. The point is that no degree of development of consciousness in terms of content, or in terms of the recognition of the subjective principle, has any effect upon the pure principle of Consciousness per se.

8 ... *When consciousness of objects is born, then,
likewise, consciousness of absence of objects arises.*

To be able to cognize any thing or object implies
the isolation of it from that which it is not. While the
degree to which this is accomplished does vary, yet the
isolation must have proceeded to some discernible
degree before an object can exist, either for thought or
perception. Where an object is completely defined,
the isolation is perfected. In that case, the universe of
discourse is divided into two classes, i.e., the class of
those instances that fall within the limits of the definition and the class of those that fall outside. But always,
in order to form any definition, there must be a cognizance of the excluded class as well as of the included
class. This is a process that proceeds continuously on
the part of all individuals whose consciousness is concerned with objects in any sense, even in the case of
those with whom the process lies very largely in the
background, where it is more or less 'unconscious' or
'subconscious.'

To have reached the point in the evolution of consciousness such that the cognition of the class of all
possible objects, in any sense whatsoever, is born, is
also to have attained at least a shadowy awareness of
absence of objects, in every sense, as a state or condition that stands in contrast. This awareness of the
absence of objects, in its purity, is not a cognition of an
object, but another form of consciousness that is not
concerned with objects. However, a reflection of this
state of consciousness may be produced so that a special cognition arises, of such a nature that its content
is definable as the inverse of all objects. This produces
a sort of ideal world that is neither the universe of objects, proper, nor Nirvana, but one that partakes, in

some measure, of the nature of both. This sort of ideal creation is very well illustrated in mathematics in connection with the development of the notions of negative, imaginary, infinitesimal, and transfinite numbers. All these may be regarded as of the nature of inverse cognitions. But they are not, therefore, cognitions devoid of meaning; however, their meaning is of a more transcendental and ineffable nature than that which is connected with the original positive real numbers, particularly the integers, which have been significantly called the natural numbers. These inverse numerical cognitions have been not only valuable but, in some respects, even necessary for the development of certain phases of western culture. They are unquestionably significant.

Now, when the awareness of the absence of objects has become embodied in a sort of inverse concept, the latter has a different kind of meaning as compared with that of the direct cognitions from which they rose genetically. This meaning stands in purely symbolic relationship to the inverse cognitions and lies outside the definitions, in a sense and degree, which is not true of the meaning of the direct cognitions, where the meaning in some degree or some sense lies within the definition. There is a sense in which we may say that we comprehend the direct cognitions with their meanings in a nonmystical manner, but in the case of the inverse cognitions the meaning is realized only through mystical insight. If, however, the inverse cognitions are interpreted as comprehensions in the nonmystical sense, then we have merely created a subtle subuniverse of objects, with the consequence that the consciousness-principle has not destroyed its bondage to objects, as such, but merely sublimated the field of objects. None the less, such sublimation may very well mean progress toward true Liberation. It may serve very much like a scaffolding, from the upper platform of which the step to true Liberation may be much facilitated.

The kind of consciousness symbolized by the system of inverse objects is of a totally different quality from anything entering into ordinary relative consciousness. It is an ineffable State of the type realized in the higher mystical states of consciousness or in Samadhi.

9 . . . Consciousness of objects is the Universe.

In one sense, this aphorism may be viewed as a definition of what is meant by the term "Universe." It is that domain of consciousness wherein a self is aware of objects, the latter standing as opposed to, or in contradistinction to, the self that is aware of them. In this sense the Universe is much more than that which is connoted by the term "physical universe," since it includes as its field, in addition to waking physical consciousness, the fields of all dream objects, of all objects of the type that psychologists call "hallucinations" or hypnogogic visions, and of any other objects that may be experienced during objective life or after death that there may be. In this sense, the psychical states in which the phantasies, so called, are experienced are classed as part of the Universe.

Since the whole field of western science is restricted to the study of the objects of consciousness, it can never extend into that realm of consciousness that is other than the universe. This science takes as its most primary base of operation the subject-object relationship in the structure of consciousness. This fact, at once, defines the limits of its field of possible action. Such delimitation does not exclude the possibility that science, in the western sense, may develop without limit in the particular dimension defined by the subject-object relationship, but this science, as such, is forever excluded from the dimensions of consciousness not conditioned by the subject-object relationship. Nor is science capable of critical evaluation of its own base, as this base is the original 'given' with which it starts and is implied in its own criticism. Competent criticism of this base is possible only from that perspective that is freed from exclusive dependence upon the subject-object relationship.

10 . . . Consciousness of absence of objects is Nirvana.

Here it is necessary to employ a Sanscrit term to suggest a meaning for which no western term seems to exist. By "Nirvana" is meant a somewhat which has been peculiarly baffling to western scholars, as is revealed in the preponderant portion of the discussion of this notion. The reason for this is not hard to find. It lies in the typically intense and exclusive polarization of the western mind toward the *object* of consciousness. Even western mystics have rarely attained a degree of subjective penetration sufficient to reach the genuine Nirvanic State. Western subjectivity scarcely means more than a domain of subtle objects, even with most of the mystics, and this is a domain still within the range of meaning of "Universe," as defined in the last aphorism.

Etymologically, "Nirvana" means "blown-out," and this, in turn, carries the popular connotation of annihilation. It is true that it does mean annihilation in a sense, but it is the annihilation of a *phase* or *way* of consciousness, not of the principle of consciousness, as such. A careful study of the Buddhist canon reveals quite clearly that Gautama Buddha never meant by "Nirvana" the destruction of the principle of consciousness, but only of consciousness operating in a certain way.

As employed in the present aphorism, "Nirvana" means that state of consciousness wherein the self does not stand in the relation to objects such that the self is to be contrasted to, and aware of, objects. Only one part of the meaning of "Nirvana" is suggested in this aphorism, i.e., that "Nirvana" designates the consciousness wherein there is absence of objects. Yet the subject to consciousness is not here supposed annulled in the deeper sense. Something of this quality of consciousness, but generally not in its purity, is to be found even in western mysticism. It is revealed in the expressions of the mystics, wherein they report realization of identity between themselves and content of consciousness. This content is so often mixed with an objective meaning that the mystical states in question must be judged as not pure, but rather, a blend of a degree of the Nirvanic State with the typical consciousness of the universe of objects. Yet always, with the mystic, there is an ineffable substratum that he never succeeds in more than suggesting in his expression. Often his effort to do justice to this substratum leads to formulation that simply does not make sense, when judged by the canons of subject-object language. The result is that only a mystic really understands another mystic.

The ineffability of the genuinely mystical consciousness is not due to an imperfect knowledge of language on the part of the mystic. While many mystics have had a very defective knowledge of language, and are consequently especially obscure, yet others have not been so limited in their equipment. However, in either case, the ineffable and obscure element remains. The fact is, this ineffability can never be conveyed through language, any more than an irrational number can be completely equated to a rational number. All our language, as such, is based upon the subject-object relationship. Thus, consciousness that transcends that relationship cannot be truly represented through language built upon that base. Therefore, the expressions of the mystics must be regarded as symbols, rather than as concepts that mean what they are defined to mean and no more.

The pure Nirvanic State of Consciousness is a Void, a Darkness, and a Silence, from the standpoint of relative or subject-object consciousness. But taken on its own level it is an extremely rich state of consciousness that is anything but empty. It cannot be conceived, but must be realized directly to be known.

11 . . . Within Consciousness-without-an-object
lie both the Universe and Nirvana,
yet to Consciousness-without-an-object
these two are the same.

Superficially considered, nothing may seem more incomprehensible than a state of consciousness from which two dissimilar states, such as the Universe and Nirvana, have the same value. But actually, the difficulty is not so great when once analysis has led to the realization that consciousness, as such, is unaffected by superimposed states or forms. Neither the Nirvani nor the man in the Universe is outside of Consciousness, as an abstract and universal principle. If a conception from mathematics may be borrowed, it may be said that the Universe and Nirvana have the same *modulus* but are different in *sense*. The notions of "modulus" and "sense," as employed in mathematics, have the following meaning: In the series of positive and negative numbers we have an unlimited number of pairs of numbers having the same absolute magnitude, but of opposite signs.[2] In this case, it is said that the members of such pairs have the same modulus but are opposite in sense. Applying this analogy, the modulus that is common to both the Nirvanic State and to consciousness in the Universe is the common quality of being *Consciousness*. The difference in "sense" refers to the opposed qualities of being objectively polarized, in the case of consciousness in the Universe, and subjectively polarized, in the Nirvanic State. Now, when the "modulus" of a number alone is important, then the positive and negative "sense" of the number is irrelevant, and therefore, may be regarded as having the same significance. By applying this analogy, the meaning of the aphorism should become clearer.

There is a profound Level of Realization wherein the two states of the Universe of Objects and Nirvana, instead of seeming like forever separated domains, become interblended coexistences. In other words, at that Level of Recognition, consciousness of objects and consciousness of absence of objects are known to be mutually complementary states, the one dependent upon the other, just as the notion of negative numbers is dependent upon the notion of positive numbers, and vice versa. And just as the student of mathematics very soon reaches the point where the notion of number, as such, comprehends the positive and negative "sense" of number, so that he no longer thinks of two distinct domains of number, so, also, is it at that higher Level of Recognition. Nirvana and the Universe of objects are simply phases of a more ultimate Reality.

Consciousness-without-an-object is not simply consciousness of absence of objects. It is THAT which is neutral with respect to the presence or absence of objects. As such, IT stands in a position of Indifference to this presence or absence. In contrast, the consciousness of absence has a positive affective quale, just as truly as is the case with the consciousness of presence of objects, and this is not a state of indifference. The actuality of positive affective quale both during presence and absence may be noted by studying the effect produced after the performance of a fine musical composition. If a period of silence is allowed to follow the performance, and the listener notes the effects upon his consciousness, he will find that there is a development of musical value in that silence. Actually, this value has a greater richness for feeling than the music had as audible sound. Further, that silence is not like any other silence, but on the contrary has an affective quale that is specifically related to the particular composition that has been rendered. We may call this the nirvanic aspect of the given musical selection. Now Nirvana, as a whole, stands in analogous relationship to the totality of the Universe of Objects. The Universe of objects is an affective privation, which becomes a corresponding affective richness in the Nirvanic Aspect. Also, the form-bound knowledge of the Universe of Objects becomes the free-flowing Gnosis, having inconceivably rich noetic content. But Consciousness-without-an-object stands in neutral relationship to both these aspects.

In the strict sense, from the standpoint of Consciousness-without-an-object, objects are neither present nor absent. Presence or absence has meaning only from a lower level. The older notion of space, as being that which is affected neither by the presence nor absence of bodies, suggests the idea.

12 . . . Within Consciousness-without-an-object lies the seed of Time.

Although consciousness-as-experience is time bound, Consciousness, as such, is superior to time. That this is so is revealed in the fact that intellectual consciousness has been able to isolate and cognize time, and then, in turn, analyze it into its component parts as past, present, and future. This is further evidenced in analytic mechanics wherein time appears as a contained conception. It is impossible to analyze that which is superior to the level on which, in a given case at a given time, the consciousness-principle is operating. The roots of any mode or form of consciousness are dark with respect to that particular mode or form. If, at any time, consciousness becomes aware of those roots and succeeds in analyzing them, it is of necessity implied that the principle of consciousness has risen to a perspective superior to the mode of consciousness in question. Thus, while consciousness-as-experience is time bound, yet, as thought, it has risen to a level where it can apprehend the time-binding roots. In this instance, we do not have to call upon the deeper mystic states of consciousness to reach to the necessary superiority of level. It is to be found in philosophy and theoretical mechanics. This is enough to show that Consciousness, as such, is not time bound, but only consciousness-as-experience.

Time is thus to be regarded as a form under which certain modes of consciousness operate, but not as an external existence, outside of consciousness in every sense. This idea is sufficiently familiar since the time of Kant not to require extensive elaboration. In the terms of Kant, time is a transcendental form imposed upon phenomena. But, it follows, consciousness, in so far as it is not concerned with phenomena, is not so bound.

The "seed of Time" may be thought of as the possibility of time. Time is an eternal possibility within Consciousness-without-an-object. Time is not to be thought of as something suddenly brought to birth, for the notion of "suddenly" presupposes time. On the time-bound level, time is without conceivable beginning or end. It is in the deeps of consciousness that time is transcended. It is quite possible so to penetrate these deeps that it is found that no difference of significance attaches to the notions of an "instant of time" or "incalculable ages of time." Yet, all the while on its own level, time continues to be a binding form. We have here one of the greatest of mysteries.

Through time it is possible to reconcile judgments that would otherwise be contradictory. This principle is so familiar as not to require elucidation. But he who reaches in Recognition to Consciousness-without-an-object finds that the logical law of contradiction no longer applies.[3] Judgments that otherwise would stand in contradictory relationships are brought into reconciliation without the mediation of time. This is an even greater mystery than the mystery of time.

13 . . . When awareness cognizes Time then knowledge of Timelessness is born.

This aphorism exemplifies another application of the principle that governs the action of consciousness that was discussed in the commentary on aphorism number 8. We are able to recognize time as a distinct form only when we are able to isolate it from what it is not. This is done not only in philosophy, but, as well, in many of the theoretical constructions of science. In these cases, however, we have an isolation for thought. The immensely important philosophical question then arises as to how far, or in what way, a necessity or possibility for thought or for reason is likewise an actuality. This question is so fundamental that it seems advisable to discuss it at some length.

The issue involved here is essentially identical with that present in the ontological argument for the existence of a Supreme Being. This argument is based upon the assumption that the existence of an idea implies the existence of a reality corresponding to it. Hence the idea of a Supreme Being implies that such a Being is. The analysis to which Kant submitted this argument is a classic in philosophical criticism, and it is generally felt that Kant has, once for all, undermined the force of this argument. Yet, despite all this, it continues to have psychological force and has reappeared more than once since Kant's time.

The aphorisms and the philosophy surrounding them do not make use of the notion of a Supreme Being, though they leave open the possibility of evolved Beings that may very well be regarded as God-like when contrasted to man.[4] But this philosophy establishes its base upon the reality of a Transcendental Principle. Hence, the essential problem involved in the analysis of the ontological argument arises here. So, to bring this question out into clear form the following quotation is taken from Kant:

Our conception of an object may thus contain whatever and how much it will; nevertheless we must ourselves stand away from the conception, in order to bestow existence upon it. This happens with sense-objects through the connection with anyone of our perceptions in accordance with empirical laws; but for objects of pure thought there is no sort of means for perceiving their existence because it is wholly *a priori* that they can be known; our consciousness of all existence, however, belongs altogether to a unity of experience, and an existence outside this field cannot absolutely be explained away as impossible. But it is a supposition we have no means of justifying.

Let us, for the present purpose, assume the general validity of this argument. Then, in simple terms, the conclusion reached is that for an object of the reason or thought to have, or correspond to, an existence, in any other sense, that existence must be determined through some other mode of consciousness. In the case of experience, the senses perform this necessary function, in that sense-impression is necessary to determine experiential existence. At the close of the quotation, Kant admits that the possibility of a non-experiential existence cannot be denied, but goes on to say that we have no means of justifying this supposition. Now, so far as the field of consciousness that is the proper field of physical science is concerned, Kant's conclusion seems to be valid enough. But the domain of consciousness comprehended by science is only a part of the sum total of all possible consciousness. Once this is granted, then, in principle, it must be admitted that the supposition of a nonexperiential or transcendent existence or reality can possibly be justified. Epistemological logic does not rule out this possibility; it simply establishes the point that by means of pure conceptions and logic alone, transcendental existences or realities cannot be proved.

In the present philosophy, all effort to establish such a proof is abandoned. Logic and analysis of consciousness are employed simply to build a reasonable presumption, without laying any claim to coercive demonstration. It is, however, asserted that direct extralogical and extraempirical verification is possible. All this implies that there is a way of consciousness that is not, on the one hand, to be regarded as presentation through the senses, or in the form of conceptions, on the other. Nor, further, is it to be regarded as no more than affective and conative attitude. It is, rather, a way of consciousness that sleeps in most men, but has become awakened and active in the case of a small minority, which is to be found represented by individuals scattered thinly throughout the whole span of history. This way of consciousness has been known by different designations, but in the West it is most commonly called "mystical insight."

In introducing this notion of another way of consciousness, called "mystical insight," certain obvious difficulties arise, owing to its not being a commonly active mode of consciousness. The individual in whom this insight is sleeping is necessarily quite incapable of evaluating it directly. To be sure, he may study the phenomena connected with the mystical function, as exemplified in historic personalities, as has been done by some psychologists. But this is a very different matter from the direct epistemological evaluation of the noetic content of the mystical insight.[5] A work like that of Kant's *Critique of Pure Reason* can be accomplished only by a man who finds in the operation of his own consciousness the very contents that he is analyzing. The study of the forms and processes of consciousness is, of necessity, only in subordinate degree a matter for observation. In the present case it depends preeminently upon the introceptive penetration. As a result, the psychologist, who is not himself also a mystic, is not competent in this field, for he of necessity judges from the base of a consciousness operating through the senses and the forms of the intellectual understanding alone, so far as cognitive content is concerned. Recognizing this difficulty, I have abandoned in the present work the effort to force agreement by means of logic and reference to a widely common ground of experience.

However, the *possibility* of a noetic insight must be indicated. The chapter on "A Mystical Unfoldment" was introduced early in this work to meet that need. Admittedly the reader is in a difficult position when it comes to the question of evaluation of the honesty and competency of the writer in the forming of his interpretations in this chapter. But there simply is no way of presenting the material and processes of mystical insight in terms that are generally objective. The record of historic instances of mystical insight that have led to the formulation of a noetic meaning adds to the presumption of the validity of the insight, but does not help the reader directly unless, he too, has known at least some modicum of the mystical sense. Consequently, all that can be asked of the general reader is that he entertain the idea of the possibility of mystical insight, and then judge the philosophic consequences from that base.

It is predicated here that one important consequence, which does follow, is that an existence or reality outside the field of experience through the senses can be justified directly without falling into the error of the ontological argument. It would follow that Kant's *Critique of Pure Reason* is, in principle, valid only with respect to the relationship between the understanding and the material given empirically through the senses. But mystical insight gives another order of material or viewpoint that, also, in combination with the understanding, has noetic value. Undoubtedly there are problems concerning possibly valid and false interpretations here, analogous to those that arise in the relationship between understanding and experience through the senses, that Kant treated so trenchantly. But only the mystic who is also a critical philosopher could possibly be qualified to handle these. In this domain Kant hardly seems to qualify, for his is the scientific, rather than mystical, mind.

Once it is granted that there are two domains from which the material filling of conceptual consciousness may be derived, instead of the one through the senses alone, then the field of cognition has a threefold, instead of a twofold, division. There would then be the domain of pure understanding or conceptual thought in a sort of neutral position, with material through the senses standing on one side, and material or viewpoint from mystical insight on the other. This, in turn, would lead to something like a division in understanding, which may be called the higher and lower phases of intellection. Another consequence is that some men may have the lower phase of intellection, that operates in connection with the material given through the senses, developed in high degree, and yet remain quite blind to the higher phase. More than extensive scholarship or superior scientific ability is required to awaken recognition of the higher phase. On the other hand, there is a considerable dearth of superior intellectual training among those who are, in some measure, awakened to the higher phase of intellection, though history affords us some brilliant exceptions. Thus, there are not many who realize that here, too, is a problem for critical philosophy.

In any case, the aphorisms must be taken as material derived from mystical insight. As a consequence, their verification in the full sense is possible only from the perspective of a similar insight. Logic and experience can provide only a partial presumption for them, at best, and that is all that is attempted in these commentaries.

14 . . . To be aware of Time is to be aware of the Universe, and to be aware of the Universe is to be aware of Time.

This aphorism emphasizes the interdependence of consciousness under the form of time and of consciousness of objects. Formerly, in the days when our scientific thought was governed by the Newtonian mechanics, we were in the habit of regarding time, space, and matter as three independent existences. Explicitly, Newton held the view that these three were not interdependent. However, as knowledge of the subtler phases of physical nature has grown, it has become evident that this view is no longer tenable. The new relativity, which has been largely developed through the insight and coordinating thought of Albert Einstein, definitely asserts the interdependence of these three notions of time, space, and matter. Now, while this integrating conception was developed to unify actually existent knowledge of physical fact, it is, at the same time, the formulation of a profound metaphysical principle. The notion of time is meaningless apart from the notion of change. Further, there is no change save in connection with objects. Thus, at once, it should become clear that awareness of objects implies change, and consequently, time, while on the other hand time becomes existent only in connection with objects.

It should be clearly understood that the ground on which this aphorism is based is not the above theory of mathematical physics, but is genuinely transcendental. However, the physical theory is a beautiful illustration of the essential idea.

15 . . . To realize Timelessness is to attain Nirvana.

In this work the terms "realize" and "realization" are used in a special sense, which is to be clearly distinguished from "perception" and "conception." Whereas the latter two terms refer to a relationship between a self and objects, whether in the form of sense objects or ideas, the terms "realize" and "realization" are employed to designate a mode of consciousness wherein there is identity between the self and content, in other words, a state of consciousness not concerned with objects in objective relation. Thus "realization" means a mystical state. The Nirvanic State is not something conceived or perceived, though it is possible to conceive or perceive a symbol that means the Nirvanic State. If the latter possibility did not exist, it would be impossible to say anything at all in reference to Nirvana.

The realization of Timelessness should not be confused with the concept of timelessness that frequently occurs in philosophy, nor with the notion of simultaneity that is employed in classical theoretical mechanics. In the case of the mere concept of timelessness, the thinking and experiencing self is actually, in terms of awareness, moving within the time-world of objects. Thus his creating of the concept is a time-process. In this case, the self is not fused into identity with that which it has conceived. But when genuine realization has been attained, the self is found identical with Timelessness. The difference here is of crucial importance, though one that is difficult to convey adequately with ideas. Not only is it not merely "knowledge about," but it is an even more intimate state than "knowledge through acquaintance, such as that which comes through immediate experience. It is, rather, a state of "knowledge through Identity." This consciousness has a peculiar quality that is quite ineffable, but it may be suggested in the following way: If we may regard all concepts and percepts as being a sort of "thin" consciousness of surfaces only, then the state of realization would be like a "thick"—substantial—consciousness extending into the "depth" dimension. All presentation and representation deal with surfaces only, and all expression in its direct meaning is solely of this nature, whatever its symbolic reference may be. But the realization gives "depth-value" immediately. It may, therefore, be called substantial in a sense that may never be predicated of mere presentations or representations. This "depth-value" actually feeds that which some modern psychologists have called the "psyche." On the other hand, mere experience and intellection do not supply this nutritive value. They may arouse self-consciousness and afford something that has the value of control, but they do not themselves give sustenance.

To attain the Nirvanic State is to reach the source of sustenance for the psyche. This is the genuine goal of the religious effort, however inadequately that goal may be envisaged in the majority of religious conceptions and programs. Religion is concerned with the sustenance of the psyche; it is a search for a durable "Manna."

To realize Timelessness is to transcend the tragic drama of Time. Time is tragic because it destroys the beloved object, and because it is constantly annulling the unused possibilities. In the Timeless State there is none of this tragedy; hence it is a State of Bliss without alloy. But Bliss without alloy is simply another name for Nirvana.

16 . . . But for Consciousness-without-an-object
there is no difference between
Time and Timelessness.

This is another instance wherein the meaning is
more easily seen by consideration of the fact that
Consciousness as a principle is unaffected by the nature of content or state. But this is not the whole
meaning of the aphorism, for Consciousness-without-
an-object is not merely an analytic abstraction from
the totality of common consciousness. It is also a symbol of That which may be directly realized. On the
level of That, there is no differentiation of Significance. In other words, it is neutral with respect to
Meaning as well as to affective value. It is a level above
all relative valuation, both in the affective and noetic
sense. Stated in another way, all differentiation has
the same significance, and this significance is simply
irrelevancy.

Consciousness-without-an-object represents all possibilities, but is specifically identified with no particular
possibility. If IT were especially close to any one tendency, then IT would cease to be perfectly neutral.
Thus all judgment or valuation lies on some lesser
level, wherein the principle of relativity operates. But
this lesser level depends upon the superior for its
possibility and existence.

17 . . . Within Consciousness-without-an-object
lies the seed of the world-containing Space.

"Space" is a generic concept, as there are many kinds
of space. Thus the perspective-space of the eye has
characteristics quite different from those of the space

with which the engineer works. The latter is generally the familiar Euclidian space. But, whereas we formerly thought that the Euclidian space was the sole real space, today we know there are many kinds of space. Most of these exist only for mathematics, but within our own day we have seen one of these purely mathematical spaces become adapted to the uses of mathematical physics. So, now the notion of a multiplicity of types of spaces is definitely extended beyond the domain of pure mathematics.

In the present aphorism, the reference is to the space in which all objects seem to exist. In the broadest sense, this is not a single space, but several sorts of spaces, all having in common the property of containing objects. Two of these spaces that are generally familiar are: (a) the ordinary space of waking consciousness, in which all physical bodies from the stars to the electrons rest; and (b) the spaces of the dreamworld, wherein distance takes on quite a different meaning. It is characteristic of these spaces, at least as far as we are commonly familiar with them, that distance and quantity are significant notions. Such notions, however, are not essential to space as such, as is revealed in the mathematical interpretation of space as "degrees of freedom."[6]

Space is to be regarded as the framework or field of each particular level of differentiated consciousness. The world-containing space is that framework in which objects appear. The normal framework of the space of waking consciousness vanishes for the dream-state, and a space having discernibly different properties replaces it. The latter is a space filled with objects quite distinguishable from the objects filling the space of waking consciousness, even though they may be related. Different laws or relationship and operation apply.

The superiority of consciousness to a specific space

is revealed in the fact that the external space of waking consciousness can be annulled by the simple act of going to sleep. The dream space is annulled by the reverse process of waking to the external space. This fact, which is part of the common experience of all men, is of profound significance, for it reveals the overlordship of the principle of consciousness with respect to these two kinds of space. It is a constant reminder that, in reality, man as a conscious being is not bound to the space that defines the form of his experiencing or thinking while in a particular state. The delusion of bondage is truly a sort of autohypnosis, produced through man's predicating of himself as a subjective consciousness-principle those spatial dependencies that apply only to objects, including his own body. In reality, the consciousness-principle supports and contains the universe, instead of the reverse being true, as commonly supposed.

The world-containing space is derived from, and is dependent upon, Consciousness-without-an-object. The latter comprehends the former, both as potentiality and as actuality.

18 . . . When awareness cognizes the world-containing Space then knowledge of the Spatial Void is born.

As the underlying principle of the complementary or inverse awareness has already been discussed in the commentaries on aphorisms 8 and 13, it will not be further considered here. Our attention will be devoted to the meaning of the Spatial Void.

The Spatial Void stands in polar relationship to the world-containing Space. The latter is preeminently a space with content involving the notions of quantity and distance. The Spatial Void is without content and involves no notion of quantity and distance. The more qualitative spaces of mathematics suggest the idea. It is predominantly Space as Freedom, and not space as restraining and constricting form. Any differentiation that would apply here would be analogous to that which attaches to the notion of transfinite numbers, and not like the sharply bound differentia of finite manifolds.

The direct realization of Consciousness as the Spatial Void has an inconceivably lofty value. It is a state in which the lonely self has found its own other in the fullest possible sense. Symbolically expressed, it is as though the lonely self, regarded as a bare point, had suddenly been metamorphosed into an unlimited space, wherein content-value and the subject—the "I"—were completely fused and coextensive. More commonly, this is expressed as union with God. The latter statement is sound enough so long as it is understood as a symbol and does not assume an arbitrary preinterpretation. The Reality realized is Presence, in the sense of envelopment in the Eternal Other. This is the final resolution of all the problems of the tragic life in the world. It is the Terminal Value, with respect to which all consciousness concerned with objects is of instrumental significance only.

19 . . . To be aware of the world-containing Space is to be aware of the Universe of Objects.

This aphorism asserts the interdependence of our ordinary space and the objects contained within it. This involves a departure from the older Newtonian view wherein space was regarded as independent of the presence or absence of objects. While it is possible to conceive such a space, it would be a space taken in a different sense from that of the world-containing space. The view developed in the new relativity is consonant with the present aphorism, for in this latter theory matter and space are viewed as interdependent. This space is not simply an empty abstraction, but actually has what might be called a substantial quality. Thus, the very form or "properties" of the space is affected by the degree in which matter is concentrated in different portions of it. It becomes warped in the vicinity of large stellar bodies, so that the shortest distance between two points is no longer a straight line, in the old sense, but a curved line, analogous to an arc of a great circle on the surface of a sphere. Modern astrophysics has even developed the idea of an expanding space, implying therewith the possibility of a contracting space. This notion, at the very least, renders intelligible and plausible in physical terms the ancient notion of a pulsating universe on the analogy of a great breath.

Once we have the notion of a space expanding with the matter, which is coextensive with it, and the consequent possibility of its contraction in another phase of the life-history of matter, then there at once emerges the further implication of the dependence of matter-space upon a somewhat still more ultimate. For pulsation implies a matrix in which it inheres. In these aphorisms, that matrix is symbolized by Consciousness-without-an-object. The objective phase of the pulsation, that which is marked especially by the expanding of the universe, is the state of consciousness polarized toward objects. The contracting phase develops while consciousness is being progressively withdrawn from objects. This may be viewed first as the macrocosmic picture—a process in the grand cosmos. The same principle applies to the microcosmic or individual consciousness.

These two senses are not generally distinguished in these commentaries, as the latter are concerned with general principles that may be applied in either sense. Thus, what is said may be interpreted either in reference to an individualized human consciousness, or to consciousness in the more comprehensive sense.

20 . . . To realize the Spatial Void is to awaken to Nirvanic Consciousness.

This aphorism effects a further expansion of the meaning of Nirvana. The latter may be viewed as a spatial consciousness, but not in the sense of a world-containing space. Nirvanic Consciousness is not to be regarded as simply the total consciousness of the manifested universe. If such a total consciousness could be envisaged, it would be very appropriate to call it Cosmic Consciousness, and it would stand as a whole, in contradistinction to Nirvanic Consciousness. These two, Nirvanic Consciousness and Cosmic Consciousness, would contrast in the relation of polarization, analogous to the familiar polarity of subject and object. In spatial symbols, the polarity is between the world-containing Space and the Spatial Void.

Now, a more complete interpretation of the pulsation noted in the last commentary becomes possible. The expansion of the world-containing Space corresponds to contraction of consciousness in the sense of the Spatial Void, or a reduction of consciousness concerned with the Self, while there is an expansion of consciousness in the field of objects. In psychological terms, it is the predominantly extroverted phase. While in such a cosmically expansive phase, the balance of human consciousness, as of all other consciousness, is bound to be predominantly extroverted, yet particular individuals may be relatively only more or less extroverted. In this setting, the so-called introverted individuals are only relatively introverted, and cannot be predominantly introverted so long as they possess physical bodies. To become predominantly introverted is to cease to exist objectively, and thus, to have consciousness centered in the Spatial Void or Nirvana.

For most individuals the centering of consciousness in the Spatial Void is a state like dreamless sleep, in other words, a psychical state that analytic psychology has called the 'Unconscious'. In this philosophy this state is not viewed as unconscious in the unconditional sense, but is conceived as a state of consciousness that is not conscious of itself, and therefore, indistinguishable from unconsciousness from the subject-object standpoint. It is possible, however, to transfer the principle of self-consciousness into the Spatial Void, in which case it is no longer a state like dreamless sleep. But this is not an easy step to effect, as it requires a high development of the principle of self-consciousness, combined with its isolation from the object. If, in the case of a given individual, this power is sufficiently developed, beyond the average of the race, it is possible for such a one to become focused in the Spatial Void, in advance of the race as a whole. When this is actually accomplished, the individual is faced with two possibilities. Either he may then become locked in the Spatial Void, in a sense analogous to that of the binding of most men to the universe of objects, or he may acquire the power to move his consciousness freely between the world-containing Space and the Spatial Void. In the latter case, the individual's base is neither the universe of objects nor Nirvana, but lies in THAT which comprehends both these. The latter is here symbolized by Consciousness-without-an-object, which is neither introverted nor extroverted, but occupies a neutral position between these two accentuations.

21 . . . But for Consciousness-without-an-object there is no difference between the world-containing Space and the Spatial Void.

In one sense there is no difference because Space or Consciousness, in either sense, is irrelevant. From the standpoint of a profound metaphysical perspective, both are irrelevant, as the just forgotten dream is irrelevant to the consciousness of the man who has awakened from sleep. Yet, while dreaming, the dream was real enough to the dreamer. We can thus distinguish a sense in which we would say the dream is not, i.e., from the perspective of the awakened consciousness for which it has been forgotten, yet, at the same time, in another sense, for the dreamer while dreaming, the dream is a real existence. Shifting now to the highest transcendental sense, we can say that both the world-containing Space and the Spatial Void both are and are not. In the sense that from the level of Consciousness-without-an-object both the universe of objects and Nirvana are not, there is no difference between them.

It is possible for an individual to achieve a state wherein consciousness is so divided that in one aspect of that divided consciousness he realizes the irrelevance or essential nonexistence of both Nirvana and the universe of objects, while at the same time in another aspect of that consciousness he is aware of the relative and interdependent reality of these two grand phases of consciousness. The synthetic judgment from this level of dual consciousness would be: "The universe of objects and Nirvana both are and are not." There is something here that can be realized immediately, but which defeats every effort of the intellective consciousness to capture and represent in really intelligible terms, but there can be no doubt of the superior authority of the State of Realization itself, for the individual who has acquaintance with it. To be sure, intellectual dialectic may confuse and veil the memory of the immense authority of the Realization, but this veiling process has no more significance than the power of the ordinary dream to veil the judgment of the waking state. Whereas the dream is generally something inferior to the waking intellectual judgment, the Realization has a transcendent superiority with respect to the latter. But can the intellectual consciousness of the man who has had no glimpse of the Realization be convinced of this? It is certainly quite difficult for the dreamer, while dreaming, to realize the purely relative existence of his dream. Has the waking intellectual judgment a superior capacity with respect to the acknowledgment of its own Transcendental Roots?

22 . . . Within Consciousness-without-an-object lies the Seed of Law.

Consciousness-without-an-object is not Itself law bound or law determined. It is rather the Root-source of all law, as of all else. Thus, when by means of Recognition an individual self is brought into direct realization of Consciousness-without-an-object, it is found that that most fundamental of all laws, the law of contradiction, no longer applies. Here no affirmation is a denial of the possibility of its contradictory. Also, Consciousness-without-an-object is that excluded middle that is neither A nor not-A. Hence, the actuality that Consciousness-without-an-object symbolizes is unthinkable, and so in order to think toward IT, a thinkable symbol must be employed.

All law, conceived as law of nature, or of consciousness in its various forms and states, or of relationships, is dependent upon law of thought. For such states of consciousness as there may be in which there is no thought, in any sense, there is no awareness of law, and, hence, no existence of law within the content of such states. But for a thinking consciousness that contains or is associated with those states, the operation of law is realized. Thus we may regard a law-bound domain as a thought-bound domain, though such thought is not necessarily restricted to the familiar form commonly known to men. This implies, among other consequences, that there is no *universe*, save for a thinker.

23 . . . When consciousness of objects is born the Law is invoked as a Force tending ever toward Equilibrium.

The school of English Empiricism performed a fundamental service for philosophy, in a negative way, by trying to interpret the mind as an empty tablet on which uncolored impressions from objects were imprinted. The culmination of this line of thought was finally achieved by Kant when he demonstrated that the only way to avoid absolute agnosticism was through the recognition of a positive contribution by the mind itself, that is, a contribution not derived from experience, however much experience might be necessary for arousing this factor into action. Kant showed that, *pari passu* with the development of awareness of objects through the senses, there was aroused knowledge of a form within which the objects were organized as a whole of experience. This "organization as a whole of experience" is simply the principle of Law in the general sense.

The most fundamental meaning of Law is Equilibrium. For equilibrium is that which distinguishes a cosmos from a chaos. The very essence of the notions of "law" and "equilibrium" is contained in the notion of "invariant." The counternotion is that of an "absolutely formless flux." If we abstract from experience all the notion of law, then all that is left is such a formless flux, devoid of all meaning. This would be a state of absolute nescience. Therefore, the existence of any knowledge, or of any dependability in consciousness, implies the presence of law. But the moment that we apprehend an object as object, we have invoked both knowledge and dependability. This is shown in the fact that the apprehension of an object implies the subject, which stands in relation to the object. Thus, Law appears as subject-object relationship. Now, at once, the factor of Equilibrium is apparent, for opposed to the object stands the complementary principle of the subject.

Laws are not discovered in nature, considered as something apart from all consciousness. Rather it is the truth that organized nature is a product of thinking consciousness. In a profound sense, the Law is known before it is empirically discovered. This is revealed in the fact, noted by psychology, that law-formations are developed out of "phantasy" processes. In notable instances, as in the case of Riemann, a form principle was evolved as a purely phantastic geometrical construction, which several decades later supplied the form for Einstein's general theory of relativity, to which current physical experience conforms better than it does to any preceding theory. The form that a given law takes when constructed in relation to a certain segment of empiric determination may be, and generally seems to be, inadequate. However, this should not be understood as implying the merely approximate or pragmatic character of Law per se. It should rather be understood as an imperfect objective apprehension of the Law, 'known' prior to experience. The real Knowledge of Law lies somewhere in what the analytic psychologist calls the 'Unconscious'. Man is born with this hidden knowledge, which rises more or less imperfectly to the surface as an intuition. Even when scientific laws are interpreted as the product of a relative purpose, the notion of Law in the deeper sense is presupposed. For the affirmation of a productive relationship between purpose and the scientific law implies a deeper Law, whereon faith in that productive relationship rests. Even the Pragmatist rests upon a base of a nonpragmatic Assurance, however little the latter may be in the foreground of consciousness.

24 . . . All objects exist as tensions within Consciousness-without-an-object that tend ever to flow into their own complements or others.

The principle involved here is illustrated by the law in psychology known as "enanteodromia." This is the law that any psychical state tends to be transformed into its opposite. The operation of this law is most evident in the case of those individuals who are extremely one-sided, since they manifest correspondingly exaggerated reversal of phase. But the principle always operates, even in the most balanced natures, though in these cases the two phases are conjoined and function together.

The operation of the principle can be observed quite widely. Thus, growth is balanced by decay, birth by death, light by darkness, evolution by the reverse process of involution, and so on. A particularly impressive illustration is afforded by the interaction of electrons and positrons when coming into conjunction. Here we have a flow of phase into counterphase, resulting in mutual cancellation and the production of a different state of matter. The dialectic logic of Hegel is a systematic application of this principle.

No object of consciousness is stable—remaining ever the same—but is, on the contrary, a state of tension that tends to transform into its complement. Consciousness-without-an-object is the universal solvent within which the centers of tension, or objects, have their field of play. All tendency in that play is counterbalanced by its countertendency, the culminating effect being an expression equated to zero. It is the zero that symbolizes the durable Reality, or Consciousness-without-an-object. Within the field of Consciousness-without-an-object, in principle, any creative tension may be produced, but unavoidably, the countertension is invoked. This is the reason why all creativeness involves a resistance that renders every construction something more than merely what one chooses that it should be. From this there results the positive consequence that any construction, however phantastic, when taken in conjunction with its counterphase, is true, while every construction whatsoever, when taken in isolation from its counterphase, is false. Thus, if the initial construction is even the most phantastic conceivable, and as far as possible from that which is generally regarded as reality, nevertheless, if the counterphase is given full recognition, the resultant is durable Truth. While, on the other hand, if the original construction is in terms of the generally conceded objective material, and grounded in the most careful observation, but is not taken in conjunction with the counterphase, the resultant effect is a false conception and, if believed in, produces a state of real delusion. In this way, it is possible for the so-called practical and scientific man to occupy an essentially false position, while some highly introvert poet, who lives quite aloof from the so-called world of real experience and who allows the initial impulse of his imagination the greatest possible freedom, but who, at the same time, carefully regards and incorporates the counterphase of his phantasy, will render manifest profound and lasting Truth. Now, all this leads to a very important consequence, namely, that starting from any state of consciousness whatsoever it is possible to arrive at the final and durable Reality and Truth, provided that the resources of the counterphase are incorporated in the self-conscious consciousness. Thus, no particular merit attaches to that peculiarly valued phase of consciousness—the extroverted phase of the so-called practical and scientific man—as a starting point for the attainment of the Real. This base may serve as an effective starting point, but equally well, may any other. In fact, it is quite possible that some present inmate of a psychiatric institution may outdistance all the philistines in the world who pride themselves on their sanity.

25 . . . The ultimate effect of the flow of all objects into their complements is mutual cancellation in complete Equilibrium.

The illustration of the positron and the electron applies here. The state of each of these units, by itself, may be regarded as one of tension, hence one is called a positive and the other a negative charge of electricity. For such isolated charges there can be no rest, as each is driven ceaselessly toward its own complement. So long as the goal of mutual fusion is not effected, they operate as the dynamic forces that underlie the existence of ponderable matter. But because these units are in a state of tension, no ponderable matter can remain stable. It is subject to the disruption that results when the positive and negative charges are fused. The labor of these charges to gain the goal of fusion may be regarded as one aspect of the dynamic force that manifests as evolution. To such extent as the fusion is effected, visible evolution terminates and ponderable matter vanishes. The resultant of the fusion is a flash of radiation. The latter may be regarded as the Nirvanic State of matter, for the radiant state is one of freedom and equilibrium.

The radiant state of matter is just another name for light. Now, while there is a wide range of wavelength and wave rate in the known scale of light-octaves, there is one constant element that has become highly significant in modern physical theory, and that is the velocity of light. Regardless of wavelength, all light travels at uniform velocity. Here we have a fact intimately related to the principle of equilibrium—a most important invariant. When ponderable matter finally vanishes, it enters a state subject to this invariant. Wavelength is so equilibrated to wave rate that the resultant is always the same.

Now, as revealed in the modern theory of relativity, the constant velocity of light becomes determinant of the form of the physical universe. It forces the view of a finite world-containing space. While it is true that from the standpoint of consciousness-bound-to-objects the high velocity gives the impression of enormous activity, with respect to which the object-world seems relatively stable, yet, if we shift our base and place our consciousness, as it were, in the sea of radiant energy, the universe of ponderable matter has the value of violent turmoil.[7] For consciousness thus centered, the high-potential of the radiant state has the value of peace and equilibrium. Further, radiant energy, through its property of uniformity of velocity, has the effect of bounding the universe of objects.

In psychological terms, by means of the law of enanteodromia, one psychical state draws forth its opposite. Ordinarily, through the tension of these two phases the restless movement of embodied consciousness is maintained. This leads to the development of life as experience. The self is driven by problems that are essentially insoluble, but by ever striving to reach the rainbow's end of a satisfactory solution, the self is forced by those problems to the development of potential psychical powers. And when the phase and counterphase of psychical states are blended in the Self, instead of continuing in a condition like that of a dog chasing his own tail, the state of tensions is dissolved in Equilibrium. In this case, the phase and counterphase cease to exist, just as the electron and positron vanish when united, and in their place is a state of consciousness of quite a different order. Throughout mystical literature one finds an oft recurring reference to this state as one of "Light." Does this not rather beautifully complete the analogy with the corresponding radiant state of matter?

26 . . . Consciousness of the field of tensions is the Universe.

This consequence follows at once when it is realized that an object exists as a tension. Although, in the ultimate sense, every tension is balanced by its opposite phase, so the equilibrium is never actually destroyed, yet consciousness, taken in a partial aspect, may comprehend only one phase, or may be only imperfectly conscious of the counterphase. For this partial aspect of consciousness, equilibrium does not exist. The consciousness of the universe of objects, taken in more or less complete abstraction from the totality of all consciousness, is preeminently consciousness in the field of tensions. One result is that any view of a segment of the universe of objects gives an impression of development, as in some direction. The usual scientific name for this apparently directed development is "evolution," and a familiar social interpretation is called "progress." Each of these terms reveals a recognition of a tension in the field of consciousness or life that forces any present given state to change into another. The fact that this change can be described as evolution or progress implies, in addition, that some directedness that is recognizable is involved in the change.

The more common view of evolution and progress is of a form that may be called linear. By this is meant a movement that could be represented approximately by a straight-line vector, the direction being given usually not only toward the future but also inclined upward. This linear form of the interpretation seems to be sustained when the segment observed is short enough and appropriately selected. Larger segments, such as those afforded through the study of geologic records, reveal a periodicity more or less clearly, and thus make it clear that the linear interpretation must be modified. It is, in fact, a profounder view to regard the form of change as like a pulsating breath or heartbeat, one phase being the diastole, the other the systole. As a result, it is impossible to predicate "progress" of the process taken as a whole. For while an individual of the extroverted type might predicate progress as characteristic of the diastolic phase, he would be inclined to regard the systolic phase as a regression, and on the other hand, the introverted type would most likely give a reverse valuation. For, to predicate "progress," some base of valuation is, of necessity, assumed, and there is no one base common to all individual valuation. Consequently, it is possible only with respect to restricted segments of experience and from the base of particular valuation to predicate either evolution and progress or devolution and retrogression.

However, regardless of how the tendency of change may be evaluated in any given case, the common fact of experience is that objects and objective states of consciousness are subject to a tension that continually forces transformation, be the rate rapid or slow. In other words, there is no rest or balance in the universe of objects taken in abstraction. For individuals who are in the more active phase of their interests, there may be nothing profoundly distasteful in this fact, but when they begin to feel the need of stability and rest, the total significance of the universe of objects becomes tragic. These differences, probably more than anything else, afford the explanation of why some men are optimists in their attitude toward the universe of objects, while others are pessimists. This difference is also that which marks the general characteristic attitudes of youth and maturity. It should be noted that pessimism and optimism are attitudes toward a phase of consciousness, and not to be interpreted as general attitudes toward all phases.

27 . . . Consciousness of Equilibrium is Nirvana.

The idea of "Nirvana," as employed in the present exposition, is not a notion of exclusively religious significance. Unquestionably, in the historic sense, this notion has been given a predominantly religious and religio-philosophical value, but when the two following considerations are taken into account, the reason for this should become clear. In the first place, the notion is introduced to the West from the East, and the oriental focus of interest is predominantly religious. In addition, the Nirvanic State is more readily accessible to the introverted type of individual polarization in consciousness, and the typical focus of interest of the introvert is more religious than scientific. As a consequence, the full value of the notion of "Nirvana" has not so far been developed. It is significant for the scientific focus of interest, as well as the religious, and is, in fact, implied in the development of science, though in this connection it is more deeply buried in the so-called "unconscious" than is the case where the focus of interest is in the direction naturally taken by the more introverted religious type. The scientific importance of the notion is nowhere more clearly revealed than in the value the idea of "equilibrium" has for scientific thinking. The profound tendency to find equilibrium in an hypothesis, theory, or law, that is so strongly manifested in the great coordinative scientific thinkers, reveals this fact. The objective material with which science is concerned never gives the hypotheses, theories, and laws. These are actually created out of phantasy, using the latter term in the sense employed by analytic psychology. To be sure, the selection of the form of the phantastic creation is guided by a due consideration of data from experience, but it is a creative act, added to pure experience, that provides the form. Now, as one studies the various hypotheses, theories, and laws of all departments of science, a very important tendency in the selection is noted. This tendency gains its clearest and most perfect expression in mathematics and mathematical physics, but is nonetheless recognizable in the other sciences. It is the tendency to express the unification of the original collection of scientific data in the form of equations. So far has this gone in modern physics—the most fundamental of natural sciences—that the culminating statements are more and more in the form of differential equations, with sensuously conceived models occupying a progressively inferior place of importance. Now, what is the psychical significance of the equation, as such? It is simply this, that in the equation we have manifested the sense or feeling for equilibrium. So long as a segment of experience is not reduced to an equation, the state of consciousness is one of tension and restlessness, and not of equilibrium. The investigator is driven on because his current position affords no resting place, and therefore, no peace. But when an adequate equation has been found, then there is a sense of conquest, rest, and peace. There is no need in man more profound than just this. If no success in this direction were ever attained, life would become unendurable, sooner or later. The sense of hunger for the equilibrating equation is simply one phase of the hunger for Nirvana—that inner Core that sustains the whole universe of experience.

The less there is of realization of equilibrium, the more painful life becomes, and likewise, the more realization of equilibrium achieved, the greater the joy and peace. Without consciousness of equilibrium, life is only a painful battle and a storm of conflicts that leads nowhere. This is Suffering, spelled with a capital S. On the other hand, the more complete the realization of equilibrium, the less the suffering, until, in the culminating state of pure Nirvanic Consciousness, there is total absence of suffering. The great difficulty is that, whereas suffering tends to stir self-consciousness into wider and wider fullness, the State of Equilibrium tends to lull it to sleep. The latter is usually the state known as dreamless sleep, when taken in its purity. But when self-consciousness has been sufficiently developed so that it can resist the lulling effect of Equilibrium, then the purely Nirvanic State can be entered without loss of self-consciousness. This is the Great Victory, the reward for the travail of living-form down the ages.

Some writers conceive Nirvana as being like the state of the newly born infant, wherein there is little or no self-consciousness. Thus it is seen as a retreat to a purely nascent consciousness, which is much inferior to genuine adult consciousness. In this view there is a part truth and a great error. Without full self-consciousness, this state may be likened to a sort of original nascent consciousness, such as must precede the development of organized consciousness. It is entirely possible for an individual who is not sufficiently developed in the capacities of organized consciousness to sink back into such a nascent stage. Therefore, Nirvana is not the immediate Goal for immature men and women. In fact, the immature entering of the state is a sort of failure. But the situation becomes wholly different when the debt to life, in the essential sense, has been completed. When any human being has reached the stage wherein experience has been substantially exhausted as a source of vital value, when this pasture has become a desert with only a few scattered bunches of grass in isolated corners, and when, in addition, the capacity for self-consciousness has been highly developed, then the only remaining significant Path lies in or through the Nirvanic Domain of Consciousness. Nirvana, in this case, is transformed from a nascent state of consciousness to the Supreme human Goal, wherein at long last the insoluble problems of life receive a final resolution and the greatest possible richness of consciousness replaces the old poverty.

This work is not written for immature men and women. It is believed that the inherent difficulty of the
subject, when viewed from the standpoint of the intellect, will automatically serve as a means of selection,
so that only those will read and understand who are
prepared to do so. For the others—the immature ones—
there are other needs that may often, for a time, seem
to lead in quite different directions. Such are not the
special concern of the present work. Largely, instinct
and the lash of both circumstance and ambition will
perform that function that the immature still require.

But those who have attained substantial maturity,
whether in the scientific or religious direction, reach,
sooner or later, a cul-de-sac wherein further development in the old directions has only a sort of meaningless 'treadmill' value—a place wherein all action means
little more than 'mark time, march'. When this time
comes, the only hope for the avoidance of a life in
utter poverty of consciousness-values lies in a shift in
the focus of consciousness. In the end, this shift will
lead to durable and adequate results only by attainment of the Nirvanic State with full self-consciousness.

28 ... But for Consciousness-without-an-object there is neither tension nor Equilibrium.

This is true for the simple reason that Consciousness-without-an-object can never be comprehended by
any partial or fractional phase of consciousness. Any
phase implies its other, and Consciousness-without-an-
object is their mutual comprehender, or rather, the
conceptual symbol of that forever inconceivable Reality that underlies and envelops all partial aspects.
Where there is no awareness of tension, no meaning

attaches to equilibrium. Here we may think of the "equals sign" in mathematics as symbolizing equilibrium, while zero symbolizes Consciousness-without-an-object. As an actually realized consciousness the distinction here is extremely subtle, and yet of vital significance. It is very easy for the mystic to combine these two states into one and simply call them both "Nirvana." In most, but not all, literature on the subject this seems to have been done, and the result on the whole seems to have been confusing, at least to the western mind. For this treatment gives to the Reality an overly introverted interpretation, and this is quite naturally repugnant to the extremely extroverted West. On the other hand, when Consciousness-without-an-object is distinguished from the purely subjective Nirvanic phase, a kind of mathematical clarity results. The subjective and objective are then seen to inhere in a neutral and more primary principle, and thus they acquire a more thinkable perspective. In the final analysis, this means that the peculiar genius of neither the East nor the West is nearer the ultimate Reality. Both are seen to stand as partial phases of a more comprehensive whole. Each has a half-truth, which is unavoidably blended with error when taken in the partial form alone. And each must add its neglected half to its recognized half to find the ultimately durable.

29 . . . The state of tensions is the state of ever-becoming.

A state of tension is a state of instability, since it implies a tendency to become other than what it now is. Every state of relative balance that is under tension can never be permanently durable, since the ever-present tendency to break away from the balance will become actual at the first opportunity. All the balance we find in the universe is of this sort, as is easily seen by considering that the atom exists as a state of tension between the nucleus and the surrounding electrons.

Since a tension is a tendency to become other, it follows readily that a state of tension implies becoming. Nothing in the worlds of experience or thought remains permanently stable, but is ever subject to becoming something else. Some elements remain relatively stable, while others change rapidly. But every objective "invariant" is, in the last analysis, only stable in the sense that a parameter is fixed for a certain phase of mathematical analysis, while for the completed analysis, it also changes. All objective life or experience is thus a process of becoming other, and taken by itself in abstraction, it is a becoming other that leads nowhere.

30 . . . Ever-becoming is endless-dying.

That which becomes ceases to be that which it was. the flash of radiation that was born upon the coalescence of the electron and the positron implies the death of the units of ponderable matter. The acorn ceases to be as it becomes the oak. As the man comes forth, the child, that was, is no more. As a new social organization occupies the field of the present, the old society is entombed in the pages of the historic past. No form or state in the empiric field is permanent, but ever develops into something else. The passing may be as imperceptible as the changes of massive geologic transformation, or as the birth and decay of stars, yet it may be as inconceivably rapid as that of the most instable species of radium. But, in any case, all things change. This is an ineluctable law of all empiric existence.

At every moment a new child is born out of a dying past. But if the death implies a birth, it is equally true that the new birth implies death. And what is good and valued in the old dies along with the not-good and that which is not valued. So long as we are restricted to objective consciousness, this dying is a tragic finality.

31 . . . So the state of consciousness of objects
is a state of ever-renewing promises
that pass into death at the moment of fulfillment.

Because of the law of becoming, that which we wish for and work for will ultimately come forth. But also because of this same law, that which is thus brought forth will not endure. Since becoming and dying never cease, the fulfillment of the newborn is also the moment at which it begins to decay. The beloved leaves us at the moment she is found, never to be regained as just that beloved object.

With much effort we climb to the top of a high mountain, and at the very moment we have attained the heights and cry, "Eureka, I have attained the goal," at that very moment only depths reaching down into darkness loom before our vision. Only descent is possible after attaining the crowning heights. Attainment ever initiates decline.

The vitalizing current of embodied life rises up within us whispering, "Look out there and see the vision of my new promises." And we look out and behold the vision of just what we wish, the value that we have cared for so dearly. Then we move toward it. At first the travel may not be so hard, but in time we face difficulties that we must needs surmount. But the vision holds and seems well worth the effort. Yet, beyond one difficulty there lies another, and still another, mounting in ever larger and larger proportions until, finally, we can overcome only by straining our last resources. But at that moment the vision has become actual as our accomplishment. And then we say, "Aye, this is good," and we rest in contemplation of the hard-earned accomplishment. Then as we hold the object of fulfillment in our hands, feasting our heart upon it, we feel it melting in those hands, like a beautous sculpture of ice in a warm place. It melts and melts and our heart grieves, and we pray to the powers that be that this desired object of beauty shall not leave us. But all this is in vain. Despite everything it melts and melts away, until, in the end, the fulfilling object of promise is no more. And then we are cast down for a season, until once more the current of embodied life rises and bids us look forth again and see still another vision. Then, again, we proceed as before, to achieve as before, and to lose as before. So it is throughout the whole of outer life, and mayhap, a long series of outer lives.

In the end, the wandering soul after many ages learns to abandon all hope. But this hour of deep despair brings the soul close to the Eternal. Vision of another Way begins to clear.

32 . . . Thus when consciousness is attached to objects the agony of birth and death never ceases.

That birth and death are ceaseless follows from aphorisms 29, 30, and 31. But birth and death are also agony. That this is a fact, in the familiar biological sense, is very well known indeed. Creatures are generally born through suffering and die in suffering. And beyond this physical or sensuous suffering there is a more subtle suffering that envelops all becoming, whether physical or ideal. The loss of the valued object is suffering, and the dying to a world of valued objects is likewise suffering. And in travail new ideals are born. On one side of its total meaning, the whole drama of becoming is one grand symphony of agony.

The attainment of a desired object is the birth of an object for the self that seeks. But the process through which this object is born rests in a field of desire-tension. When there is desire, there is want or craving, and this is a state of suffering. Then when the desired object is born to the individual as possession, forthwith it begins to die as the no-longer-wished-for. Attainment becomes boredom. This, again, is suffering.

Attachment to objects is, in all ways, a state of suffering, lightened only briefly by satisfaction at the moment of success. But the satisfaction is born to bloom for but a fleeting moment, then to decay in the long dying of boredom. Suffering reigns supreme over the world-focused consciousness.

33 . . . In the state of Equilibrium
where birth cancels death
the deathless Bliss of Nirvana is realized.

Birth and death are strung on a continuum of Life that is not born, nor ever dies. Life does not come into being with birth, nor does it cease with death. It is the living object that is born and dies. In the end, death just equals birth, and that which underlies remains unaffected. Here Equilibrium reigns eternally and unaffected. When self-consciousness abides in the underlying Life, birth and death are realized as just cancelling each other, and so have no reality. Thus, there is no suffering, but only the eternal Bliss of undying Life. This is Nirvana.

34 ... But Consciousness-without-an-object is neither agony nor bliss.

Agony or bliss are experienced or realized states, but the experiencing and realizing inhere in pure Consciousness. The latter is unaffected by that which it contains. Like Space, It is an universal support that remains ever the same no matter what the nature of the supported may be. When self-consciousness fuses with the pure Consciousness, no longer is modification or coloring of consciousness known. Hence, there is neither agony nor bliss, but only eternal possibility.

35 ... Out of the Great Void, which is Consciousness-without-an-object, the Universe is creatively projected.

THAT, which is here symbolized by "Consciousness-without-an-object," has long been called the "Great Void." It is the "Shunyata"—Voidness—of the Buddhists, and the "Nothing" of Jacob Behmen. It is that which, when defined exactly rather than represented symbolically, is designated only by the negation of every possible predicate. But that of which only negations are strictly true can seem solely as nothing at all to relative consciousness. Hence IT has been, repeatedly, called the "Void" or the "Nothing." IT is not a possible content of any conception whatsoever. For thought, and also for sense, IT truly is Nothing. But to say, therefore, that it is nothing in every sense whatsoever is to imply that all being is necessarily a being for sense or thought. No man has the knowledge that would enable him to say, justifiably, that thought and sense comprehend all possibilities of Being; while, on the other hand, there are those who know that there is Being beyond the possibility of sense and thought. Kant implied such Being in his "thing-in-itself," and von Hartmann located it in the collective "Unconscious," while Schopenhauer called it "Will." The mystic has proclaimed it in the most ancient of literature, and reaffirmed it from time to time down to the present.

"Creative projection," as here understood, is wholly other than the theological conception of "creationism." There is here no creative act of a Deity that stands, essentially and substantially, separate from the created, nor does the creative projection produce souls *de novo*. Essentially, "creative projection" is identical with "emanation," but with the additional implication that the emanation depends upon an initial act of will, which was not necessary. That is, the act of will is not necessary in the sense that it might not have been, but necessary in the sense that without the act of will there would have been no universe. An absolutely necessary emanation would not be a creative projection.

The standpoint here is in substantial agreement with that of von Hartmann, in that the Universe as its *possibility* is predetermined by the ideas that lie in privation of form eternally in THAT, but as to its *actuality* is the effect of a free act of Will. Since the Will is free, it could have failed to will actualization. But It has so willed, and thereby invoked necessity as the law that determined the form of the Universe. Science discovers, or rather, uncovers, the necessity in the Universe, but never finds the Thatness without which there never would be any actuality whatsoever.

This creative power does not transcend man when man drives his self-consciousness to his ultimate roots. But as long as man is in a state of consciousness seemingly isolated from the Roots, he seems to be merely an effect of causes that transcend him. Hence it is only for man as isolated—as the Great Orphan—that the Divinity appears transcendent, i.e., lying at a distance. However, when man has carried self-consciousness into the ultimate Roots, he becomes, in his own right, a potential center of creative projection, and consciously so. At this inmost state of consciousness he may choose to will actualization, or may refrain from so choosing. If he chooses to will actualization, he creatively projects, in conformation with the idea that he thinks. Thus, finally, it is seen, man is his own creator.

As conscious creator, man is God-man; as the created, he is creature, in the sense long used by the mystics. In the mystic Way, the denial of creature-man is but preliminary to the realization of the God-man. Theistic preconception has led many Christian mystics to misinterpret the real meaning of the deepest phase of their realization, but they have reported the schematic pattern correctly. Actually, in the state of ultimate realization it is not Otherness—i.e., God—who replaces the man, but the true self-identity of man replaces the false image that led man to conceive himself as creature only. It is true that mystical insight is a revelation of Man, rather than a revelation of God, provided the total meaning of "man" is sufficiently deepened. But "Man," understood in this adequate sense, is as much inaccessible to objective psychology as ever was the God of the Theists.

36 . . . The Universe as experienced is the created negation that ever resists.

The creative act is entirely free or spontaneous, but the created effect is subject to the law of necessity. The creative act may be quite consciously chosen, yet the

necessity invoked may be only imperfectly understood. In this case, I find that *I* have willed more than
I knew, and thus face compulsive necessity in the environment that *I* have creatively produced. As a result,
further willing is conditioned by this necessity. Hence,
the created projection resists me. I must conform to
its conditions, though *I* was its source.

37 . . . The creative act is bliss, the resistance, unending pain.

In creativeness the stream of Life flows freely, and
the free-flowing is Joy. The Bliss of the mystic is consciousness fused with the free-flowing Life. Before
embodied life was, the free-flowing Life is. Though
embodied life seems to exist, yet the free-flowing Life
continues, quite unaffected. And when embodied life
is no more, still the free-flowing Life remains as always. The ordinary consciousness belongs to the somatic life, but the mystic consciousness is part and
parcel of the germinal Life. Creativeness is of the very
essence of germinal Life, while the somatic life is
bound by the restraint of form. The one is all-bliss, the
other all-enveloping pain. Since the consciousness of
the concrete man is mainly, but not exclusively, somatic, there are brief moments of joy in the usual life,
but pain predominates, overwhelmingly. This, any
man can see, if he looks at his empiric life objectively
and realistically without any of the coloring cast by
hope.

38 . . . Endless resistance is the Universe of experience; the agony of crucifixion.

Frustration is of the very essence of objective existence. That the consciousness of embodied man is not

wholly frustrated is due to the fact that actual ordinary consciousness is not *wholly* objective. Glimmerings from the Roots do arise from time to time, and they cast transient sheaths of joyousness over the objective field. But generally the source of these glimmerings is not known for what it is, and so the objective field is credited with value which of itself, taken in abstraction, it does not possess. The purely objective is a binder or restricter that denies or inhibits the aspiration of the soul. The creative drive from within can find room within the objective only by the rending of constricting form. Hence it is that the fresh manifestation of Spirit is always at the price of crucifixion. The birth of the Christ within man is ever at the price of rending apart the old man of the world.

39 . . . Ceaseless creativeness is Nirvana, the Bliss beyond all human conceiving.

Creativeness, taken in isolation from the created effect, is unalloyed Bliss. A Nirvanic State that is taken in complete isolation is pure Bliss, quite beyond the conception of ordinary consciousness. But this is a partial consciousness, standing as the counterpart of isolated objective consciousness. It is not the final or synthetic State, and thus is not the final Goal of the mystic Path. But it is a possible abiding place, and it is possible for the mystic to arrive in, and be enclosed by, the Nirvanic State in a sense analogous to the ordinary binding within objective consciousness. There is a sense in which we may speak of a bondage to Bliss as well as a bondage to pain. It is, unquestionably, a far more desirable kind of bondage than that in the dark field of the object, but the bound Nirvani is not yet a full Master. To be sure, he has conquered one kind of bondage, and thus realized some of the powers of mastery, but an even greater problem of self-mastery remains unresolved.

The attainment of Nirvana implies the successful meeting of all the dark trials of the Path. The struggle with personal egoism has resulted in a successful issue; the clinging to objects has been dissolved; the battle with temptations and threatening shadows along the Path has been successfully fought; and resolution has been maintained firmly; but there still remains the task of rising superior to Glory. The little appreciated fact is that the Goal of aspiration may become a possessor of the Self, and something like spiritual egoism may replace the old personal egoism.

It is easy for many to understand that dark tendencies in the soul should be overcome, for with many the light of conscience at least glows in the consciousness. These may, and generally do, find it difficult to overcome the dark tendencies. Quite commonly, we find ourselves doing that which we would not do and leaving undone that which we unquestionably feel we should do. The undesirability of such tendencies we recognize, but find difficulty in knowing how to deal with them. The better part of our innate moral sense certainly supports the discipline of the Way that leads to Nirvana. Yet beyond this there lies an unsuspected, and inherently more difficult problem.

We may think of Nirvana as the State in which all of highest excellence or value is realized, and in a form that is not alloyed with any dross. It is, indeed, the Divine Presence of the Christian mystic. It is quite natural to conceive of this as the Ultimate, beyond which there is nothing more. But there is a defect. For here is a State that I enjoy and to which I tend to cling, and thus it involves a kind of selfishness, though it is a spiritual kind of selfishness. Thus I am possessed, even though possessed by That to which I give highest value and honor.

After all, Bliss is a valued modification of consciousness. But where there is valuation there is still duality— a difference between that which is valued and that which is depreciated. The highest State transcends even the possibility of valuation, and its complementary depreciation. The Highest Perfection finds no distinction whatsoever. This is the State in which there is no Self of any sort, whether personal or spiritual, and where there is no embodiment of Supreme Values or God. It is the Vast Solitude, the Teeming Desert.

To turn one's back upon the best of everything is intrinsically more difficult than to turn away from those things and qualities that one's moral judgment and best feeling condemn readily enough. But it is not enough to arrive at the Place beyond evil; it is also necessary to transcend the Good. This is a dark saying, hard to understand, yet it is so. But he who has found Nirvana is safe.

40 . . . But for Consciousness-without-an-object there is neither creativeness nor resistance.

One might say that IT is both creativeness and resistance, but in the last analysis this is a distortion of the Reality. To be sure, IT supports both possibilities, but as directly realized IT is a Consciousness so utterly different from anything that can be conceived by the relative consciousness that only negations can be predicated of IT. As it were, the creating and the creation are simply annulled. From that standpoint it is equally true to say that the universe is and yet it is not and never has been, nor ever will be. And equally, it would have to be said that there is not, never has been, nor ever would be, any creativeness. It is quite useless to try to conceive this, since there is no substitute for the Direct Realization.

41 . . . Ever-becoming and ever-ceasing-to-be are endless action.

That ever-becoming and ever-ceasing to be are action is self-evident. But the aphorism implies more than this. It defines the nature of action. Action is not merely a moving from here to there; it is a dying of a "here" together with a birth of a "there." To act is to destroy and beget. To act is to lose that which has been, though it replaces the old with something new.

42 . . . When ever-becoming cancels the ever-ceasing-to-be then Rest is realized.

This seems self-evident, as Rest is clearly the other of all action, whether in the positive or negative sense. But one might draw the erroneous conclusion that Rest and Action exist exclusively in discrete portions of time. Actually, Rest and Action may be realized at the same time. At a sufficiently profound level of realization, ceaseless Action leaves the eternal Rest inviolate. The disjunction of these two complementaries is valid only for partial consciousness.

43 . . . Ceaseless action is the Universe.

The Universe or Cosmos is the active phase or mode of THAT of which neither Action nor Rest may be predicated, when conceived as a totality.

44 . . . Unending Rest is Nirvana.

Since Nirvana, as here understood, is ever the complementary other of the Universe, it is that which the Universe is not. Hence, with respect to Action, Nirvana has the value of Rest.

It should be clearly understood that with respect to the present aphorisms the conception of Nirvana is not necessarily identical with the definitions of the oriental usage of the term, though there is at least a considerable degree of agreement in the meanings. The term is here used to represent meanings born out of a direct Realization that may not be *wholly* identical with any other that has been formulated.

45 . . . But Consciousness-without-an-object is neither Action nor Rest.

Both Action and Rest are rooted in THAT, but of THAT as a whole neither Action nor Rest can be predicated. THAT is all embracing but unconditioned. Thus, since any positive predication is a conditioning because it defines, and gives, to that extent, a delineation of nature or character, thereby implying an Other that is different, it follows that no such predication can be valid. On the other hand, negative predication is valid if it is clearly understood that it is a restriction that is denied, and not a Power.

46 . . . When consciousness is attached to objects it is restricted through the forms imposed by the world-containing Space, by Time, and by Law.

Space, Time, and Law condition the contents of consciousness but not the consciousness itself. And when any center of consciousness is attached to, and thus identified with, contents or objects, it seems to be likewise conditioned. Thus to the extent man is so attached, he is not free but is determined. The doctrine of determinism, therefore, does express a part truth, i.e., a truth that has pragmatic but not transcendental validity. So he who feels himself wholly conditioned is highly attached. But the concrete consciousness may be in a state that is anything from slightly to highly detached, and thus have a corresponding experience of freedom, which we may view as determination through the Subject, rather than conditioning through the Object or environment. Mankind as a whole knows little genuine freedom, but lives conditioned in part by the objective environment and in part by psychical factors, which are none the less objective because of being subtle. But authentic freedom is possible.

47 . . . When consciousness is disengaged from objects, Liberation from the forms of the world-containing Space, of Time, and of Law is attained.

Disengagement or detachment from objects does not necessarily imply the noncognition of objects. But it does imply the break of involvement in the sense of a false identification with objects. It is possible to act upon and with objects and yet remain so detached that the individual is unbound. Thus, action is not incompatible with Liberation. One who attains and maintains this state of consciousness can achieve an authentically willed action.

48 . . . Attachment to objects is consciousness bound within the Universe.

The meaning here with respect to consciousness is to be understood in the sense of an individual center of consciousness, not consciousness in the abstract or universal sense. Further, it is not stated that attachment to objects produces the Universe, but simply that consciousness—in the sense of individual center of consciousness—is bound within the Universe. Thus, this aphorism does not lead to the implication that the Universe, as such, is necessarily an illusion devoid of all reality value, but rather affirms that attachment produces a phase of bondage with respect to individual consciousness. Undoubtedly this does result in a state of delusion, but this may be no more than a mode of the individual consciousness, with respect to which the judgment that the Universe, as such, is unreal would be an unjustified extrapolation.

49 . . . Liberation from such attachment is the State of unlimited Nirvanic Freedom.

That the Nirvanic State of Consciousness is one of Liberation or Freedom has long been the traditional teaching. The aphorism accentuates the fact that this Freedom depends upon detachment from the object, but does not imply that such detachment is the whole meaning of the Nirvanic Freedom. It does imply that, while realization of the Nirvanic State is dependent upon detachment from the object, it is not dependent upon noncognition of the Object. For simple cognition of the Object does not necessitate attachment to it. Thus realization of Nirvana is, in principle, compatible with continued cognition of the World, provided there is nonattachment to it.

The Nirvanic State of Consciousness when realized in its purity does imply noncognition as well as detachment from the Universe of Objects. Possibly this is the more frequent form of the realization, and there exists the view that this is the only possible form of the realization. But this is an error. If this were the truth, then Nirvana could only be a realization in a full trance of objective consciousness, or after physical death. But a more integral realization is possible, such that the Nirvanic State may be known together with cognition of, and even action in, the world, provided there is detachment. Confirmation of this may be found in several of the northern Buddhistic Sutras and in the writings of Sri Aurobindo.

Detachment is a negative condition of the realization, but positively more is required in order that the realization may reach into the relative consciousness. A new power of cognition must also be actuated, else the realization is incomplete. This new power is born spontaneously, though there may be a time lag in the adjustment of the relative consciousness. However, the aphoristic statement is not concerned with psychological detail of this sort, no matter how great may be its human importance. Actually, the aphorisms are a sort of spiritual mathematic dealing with essential relationship, rather than with the more humanistic factors.

50 . . . But Consciousness-without-an-object
is neither bondage nor Freedom.

First of all this is true for the general reason that pure Consciousness is not conditioned or determined by either or both members of any pair of opposites.

But without the pure Consciousness there could be neither bondage nor Liberation. Only because of the experience of bondage is it possible to realize Liberation; likewise, without knowledge of Freedom there could be no cognition of a state of bondage. Movement, development, or process appear to our relative consciousness as either determined by law or a manifestation of free spontaneity, but these are only alternatives of the relative consciousness and not ontological forms. To any given center of consciousness, Being may appear either as absolutely conditioned or as a freely playing spontaneity, but the fact that it so appears to such a center tells us something about the individual psychology of the latter, and does not reveal to us the nature of the Ultimate as it is in itself.

51 . . . Consciousness-without-an-object
may be symbolized by a SPACE that is
unaffected by the presence or absence of objects,
for which there is neither Time nor Timelessness;
neither a world-containing Space nor a Spatial Void;
neither Tension nor Equilibrium;
neither Resistance nor Creativeness;
neither Agony nor Bliss; neither Action nor Rest;
neither Restriction nor Freedom.

This, together with the following aphorisms, introduces an alternative symbol for Consciousness-without-an-object, i.e., the symbol of SPACE. No form, either conceptual or aesthetic, can possibly be an adequate representation of the all-containing Ultimate Reality, since such form is a comprehended or contained entity. But a form may serve as a pointer to a meaning beyond itself and thus fulfill an office in the human consciousness in the sense of orienting the latter beyond itself. The effective symbol must possess the dual character (*a*) of being in some measure comprehensible by the human consciousness, and (*b*) of reaching beyond the possibility of human comprehension. In the literature dealing with Realization many symbols may be found that have served this office. But in time, symbols tend to lose their power as the evolving human consciousness approaches a comprehensive understanding of them. Then new and more profound symbols must be found to replace the old. Consciousness-without-an-object is such a symbol for the more subjective orientation of human consciousness, while SPACE is a corresponding symbol for the more objective orientation. The notion of "Void" or "Emptiness" has been used, but has the weakness of suggesting to many minds complete annihilation, hence the more positive symbols of Consciousness-without-an-object and SPACE are used here.

"Space" is a symbol that has been used before, and one of the best explanations of it is to be found in *The Secret Doctrine*. Thus:

> The 'Parent' Space is the eternal, ever-present
> Cause of all—the incomprehensible Deity, whose
> 'Invisible Robes' are the mystic Root of all Matter,
> and of the Universe. Space is the *one eternal thing*
> that we can most easily imagine, immovable in its
> abstraction and uninfluenced by either the presence
> or absence in it of an objective Universe. It is
> without dimension, in every sense, and self-existent.
> Spirit is the first differentiation from 'THAT', the
> Causeless Cause of both Spirit and Matter. As
> taught in the Esoteric Catechism, it is neither
> 'limitless void', nor 'conditioned fullness', but both.
> It was and ever will be.[8]

"Space," as used for the symbol, is not to be identified with any of our perceptual or conceptual spaces that are conceived as having specific properties, such as three dimensional, "curved," and so on. The notion must be understood in the most abstract sense possible, as the root or base of every specifically conceivable space. Nor is it to be conceived as either "fullness" or as "voidness" but rather as embracing both conceptions. It thus is a better symbol than either "voidness" or "plenum."

But while the interpretation of THAT as either voidness or plenum is not ultimately valid, yet relative to the needs of different types of human consciousness the symbol is most effective when taken in one or the other of these two aspects. When the approach is predominantly negative with respect to relative consciousness, naturally the symbol is conceived under the form of the Voidness, as in the case of Shunya Buddhism. But in this work the accentuation is positive, and thus "SPACE" or "Consciousness-without-an-object" is conceived provisionally as substantive, with the acknowledgement that this orientation is not ultimately valid.

As the distinction between these two aspects or emphases is of considerable importance, some discussion of them may be valuable. Technically, the distinction has been given the form of Substantialism versus Nonsubstantialism. Thus, quoting from Hamilton: "Philosophers, as they affirm or deny the authority of consciousness in guaranteeing a substratum or substance to the manifestations of the Ego and Non-Ego, are divided into Realists or Substantialists and into Nihilists or Non-Substantialists."[9] It is easy to see that under the class of Nonsubstantialism also belong the philosophies classed as Positivism, Phenomenalism, Agnosticism, and Aestheticism.[10] As examples of the substantialistic philosophical orientation, particular attention may be drawn to the philosophies of Spinoza and Sri Aurobindo Ghose[11]; while as examples of non-substantialistic philosophies we may cite those of August Compte and the Taoist, and most of the Buddhist, particularly Zen Buddhism.

One fact that stands out is that the contrasting views, while quite understandably exemplified in various speculative philosophies, are also to be found among philosophies based upon realization. This may strike one with the force of considerable surprise. For, if realization is an authentic insight into Truth, should it not lead to fundamental agreement when manifested as philosophic symbols? Offhand, one may quite reasonably expect such to be the case, yet a fairly wide acquaintance with the literature reveals divergencies sufficiently wide as to appear like contradictions. Since this can be a stumbling block for the seeker, it is probably well to give the question some consideration.

One reaction to this apparent contradiction, on the part of the seeker who has attained some degree of realization, is to view those formulations that are most consonant with his own insight as revealing an authentic Enlightenment, while the incompatible statements are regarded as in essential error and thus not the expression from the matrix of a genuine Enlightenment. As a result, we may have the development of a considerable degree of separative intolerance at a relatively high level. While all this may be quite understandable as a subjective phenomenon and may serve certain psychological needs, nonetheless, objectively considered, it is less than an integral view. Or, even if the seeker does not take so extreme a position, he may view his own expression and those of similar form as necessarily the more comprehensive, while viewing opposed expressions as inferior insights. In general, such attitudes are simply not sound, for even a considerable degree of

Enlightenment is compatible with a failure to transcend one's own individual psychology. Indeed, the Transcendental Consciousness as it is on its own level is inevitably stepped down and modified by the psychological temperament of the sadakha,[12] and if the individual has not become cognizant of the relativity of his own psychology, he can very easily fall into the error of projecting his own attitude as an objective universal. Actually, opposed interpretations may be just as valid, and even more valid, and in any case, an Enlightenment that is sufficiently profound will find a relative or partial truth in all authentic formulations.

The philosophic expressions, whether Substantialistic or nonsubstantialistic, are, in any case, but partial statements, expressions of one or another facet, and are valid as long as taken in a provisional sense. One may know this and acknowledge it and then proceed with the development that accords the better with his Vision. Then there need not be any fundamental conflict with counter-, yet essentially complementary, views. Of necessity any formulation must be partial and incomplete, however wide its integration.

52 ... As the GREAT SPACE is not to be identified with the Universe, so neither is It to be identified with any Self.

The SPACE of the symbol is here called the GREAT SPACE to emphasize the fact that it is to be understood as space in the ultimate or generic sense, in contradistinction to the special spaces of perception and conception. Further, IT is neither an objective nor a subjective space and hence may not be designated as either the Self or the Universe.

53 . . . The GREAT SPACE is not God,
but the comprehender of all Gods,
as well as of all lesser creatures.

The GREAT SPACE transcends and embraces all entities, even the greatest. There is a sense in which we may validly speak of the Divine Person, but, underlying, overlaying, and enveloping even This, is THAT, symbolized by the GREAT SPACE.

54 . . . The GREAT SPACE, or
Consciousness-without-an-object, is the
Sole Reality upon which all objects
and all selves depend and derive their existence.

The essential additional affirmation of this aphorism is that the GREAT SPACE is the *sole* Reality. What this means seems evident enough until one stops to think about it, and then at once difficulties appear in both the notions "sole" and "reality." First of all, "sole" suggests the meaning of "one," which is clearly abstracted from a matrix that also embraces the notions of "many" and "plurality." In this sense, a sole reality would exclude the possibility of multiplicity, and we would still find ourselves within the dualistic field. Actually THAT must be conceived as both not many and not one, when speaking in the strictly metaphysical sense, but unless we would abandon the effort to build a thinkable and psychologically positive symbol, we must go further than purely negative definition. Actually, the symbol is a psychological value that serves the orientation of individual consciousness and thus is something less than metaphysical truth. Therefore, the accentuation of soleness or oneness is to be conceived as a corrective to the states of consciousness that lie in bondage to the sense of manyness. It is thus not an ultimate conception. However, soleness may be conceived in a sense having a higher, as well as in a sense having a lower, relative validity. So we should think of the soleness as having a unity more like that possessed by the mathematical continuum than that of the bare number "one." For the continuum is a notion of a unity of a totality composed of infinite multiciplicity but not involving relationships between discrete entities. This appears to me the best positive conception as yet possible for suggesting the Reality underlying the negative definition of "not one and not many."

With respect to the notion of "Reality," we have even greater difficulties, for whether used in the philosophic or the pragmatic senses it has had, historically, several meanings. Most commonly, at least in western thought, this notion has been employed in relation to supposed objective existences, and this is obviously not the sense that could apply to the GREAT SPACE, which is neither objective nor subjective. We must, therefore, undertake some effort to derive the meaning that is valid for the aphorism.

Ordinarily, we think of "reality" as in contrast to the notion of "illusion," but this hardly leads to a clear understanding, since each notion becomes negatively defined by the other, and we are little, if at all, advanced to a true conception of what we *feel* in relation to these notions.[13] Pragmatically, we generally have little difficulty in differentiating between many illusions and relative realities, such as a mirage lake and a real lake, but this is not enough to define for us what we mean when these terms are extended to a metaphysical usage. For clearly, as a bare, visual, sense-impression, the mirage lake is as authentic as a real lake. We might say that as aesthetic modification of consciousness the one is as real as the other, but the distinction of reality versus illusion arises when some judgment is added to the pure aesthetic modification. But a judgment does not give reality; it gives either truth or error. If the judgment produces an error, then we are obsessed by an illusion; otherwise there is no illusion.

It would appear that this identification of illusion and error leads to the conclusion that the other of illusion is not reality but truth, and this opens a door for analysis that is much more fruitful. In support of this view, attention is called to the following quotation from Immanuel Kant: "Still less can appearance and illusion be taken as identical. For truth or illusion is not to be found in the objects of intuition, but in the judgments upon them, so far as they are thought. It is therefore quite right to say that the senses never err, not because they always judge rightly, but because they do not judge at all."[14]

If the other of truth is illusion, then it at once becomes evident that the other of reality is appearance, the latter notion not implying illusion unless an erroneous judgment has been made concerning it, and in that case, the illusion has been produced by the mistaken judgment and is not a property of the appearance as such. We can now derive a meaning for "reality" that is valid with respect to the usage of the aphorism. "Reality" becomes identical with "Noumenon," and its other, "appearance," with "phenomenon." With this the distinction becomes epistemologically defined and acquires a certain clarity of meaning.

In the history of western thought the most important development of the contrasting conceptions of "Noumenon" and "phenomenon" has been in the Greek philosophies and the philosophy of Immanuel Kant. The meanings given in these two usages, while

fundamentally related, are not identical; a result growing out of the critical thinking of later times. With
Plato, in particular, the noumenon designates the intelligible, or the things of thought, but which are not
objects for sensibility. The latter are phenomena and
are of an inferior and even undivine order. With Kant,
the noumenon is generally equivalent to the thing-in-
itself as it is in abstraction from the intuition of the
senses, while the phenomenon remains, as it was with
the Greeks, the sensibly given object. But unlike the
Greeks, Kant did not view the noumenon as an
existence given through the pure reason. Pure thought
might find it a necessary or useful conception but did
not, by itself, give it existence. What Kant has to say
here is quite valuable as pointing to a conception that
is of fundamental importance in the present work, and
accordingly, the following quotation is worthy of
special attention.

In the Critique he says: If I admit things
which are objects of the understanding only, and
nevertheless can be given as objects of an intuition,
though not of sensuous intuition . . . such things
would be called Noumena. . . . Unless, therefore, we
are to move in a constant circle, we must admit
that the very word phenomena indicates a relation
to something the immediate representation of
which is no doubt sensuous, but which nevertheless,
even without this qualification of our sensibility
(on which the form of our intuition is founded),
must be something by itself, that is, an object
independent of our sensibility. Hence arises the
concept of a noumenon, which, however, is not
positive, nor a definite knowledge of anything, but
which implies only the thinking of something
without taking any account of the form of sensuous

intuition. But, in order that a noumenon may signify a *real* object that can be distinguished from all phenomena, *it is not enough that I should free my thought of all conditions of sensuous intuition, but I must besides have some reason for admitting another kind of intuition besides the sensuous,* in which such an object can be given, otherwise my thought would be empty, however free it may be from contradictions.[15]

Kant's significant addition to the Greek conception is the statement that if the noumenon is to be realized as real, and thus more than a formal conception, there must be an intuition of it other than sensuous intuition. This is clearly the intellectual intuition of Schelling and other subsequent philosophers. In the present system such a function is affirmed but has been called "introspection," for reasons to be discussed in a future volume.

At last we are in a position to define "Reality" as the noumenon that is immediately cognized by Introception, or Knowledge through Identity, while "phenomenon" means the sensuous appearance. A third form of cognition would be conceptual representation that occupies a position intermediate between the phenomenon and the noumenon. But we must take a further step, since the Subject or Self, neglected by the Greeks and treated as a constant by Kant, becomes for us a component that is constant and primary only in relation to the object, but in relation to Pure Consciousness is derivative. We might view this Subject as a sort of transcendental phenomenon, i.e., transcendental with respect to the object but standing in something like a phenomenal relationship to Pure Consciousness.

55 . . . The GREAT SPACE comprehends both the Path of the Universe and the Path of Nirvana.

Essentially this aphorism is a reassertion of previous formulations in terms of Consciousness-without-an-object. The two Ways of the Subjective and the Objective are embraced in the one Way of the universal and transcendental comprehender. A consciousness that is sufficiently awakened would find Nirvana and the Universe to be coexistences capable of simultaneous realization.

56 . . . BESIDE THE GREAT SPACE THERE IS NONE OTHER.

1. The Subject or Self occupies a position analogous to that of the parameter in mathematics. In simple and general terms, the parameter may be thought of as a local invariant that varies when considered over a larger domain. With respect to a specific case of a given curve, it stands as the invariant element, but in the generation of a whole family of curves of a given type, it is a variable. The ultimate invariant is the plane or space in which the curves lie. This supplies us with a thinkable analogue.

With respect to a specific entity, the invariable identity is the Self, but with respect to all creatures and all modes of consciousness, the Self becomes a parameter that varies. Behind and supporting this parameter is the ultimate invariant, Pure Consciousness Itself. Herein we have a key for the reconciliation of the Atmic doctrine of Shankara and the anatmic doctrine of Buddha. Esotericism states that the Atmic doctrine was a "stepped down" formulation of the Buddha's doctrine and thus was more easily assimilated by relative consciousness, whereas the pure Buddhist doctrine was well-nigh completely incomprehensible without a preliminary re-orientation of human consciousness.

2. These are the plus and minus signs.

3. Anyone who has read any considerable amount of mystical literature can hardly fail to be impressed with the frequent affirmations and denials of the same predicate. Often an assertion made is immediately denied, or a counter assertion is made that logically implies the negation of the first. The effect is naturally confusing and can, quite understandably, lead the reader to question the sanity of the writer. But the fact is that the mystic is seeking a formulation that is true with respect to his realization, and he finds that his first statement, while partly true, is also a falsification. The denial or counter assertion is then offered as a correction. Too often the reader is offered no rational explanation and is left to draw his own conclusions, which are all too likely to be unfavorable to the mystic and to mysticism as such. And, indeed, what is the good of a statement if one cannot depend upon it so as to draw valid conclusions that can be different from other ideas that are not true to the meaning intended? Or, if the credibility of the mystic is not questioned, then it may be concluded that the reality the mystic is reporting is a sort of

irrational chaos, something quite incompatible with the notions of harmony, order, and equilibrium—a somewhat that not only defeats all possible knowing but is quite untrustworthy as well.

Now the fact is, the Gnostic Reality is not a disorderly chaos but is of such a nature that a valid representation cannot be given in our ordinary conceptual forms. These ordinary forms come within the framework of the logic of identity, or otherwise stated, the logic of contradiction. The primary principle here is classification in the form of the dichotomy, i.e., all things are either A or not-A. There is implied the exclusion of all that is neither A nor not-A, or is both A and not-A. This is known in logic as the principle of the "excluded middle," and is employed considerably in reasoning with respect to finite classes. But this is by no means our sole logical principle employed in scientific thought. Thus, mathematics requires the use of logical forms that cannot be reduced to the logic of identity, nor is this adequate for problems dealing with processes of becoming, as in organic evolution. As a consequence, there are logicians who seriously question the universal validity of the principle of the excluded middle. Thus it appears to be unsound when applied to infinite classes, as in the case of the transfinite numbers. As a consequence, then, the mystic may well be justified in his effort to get around the excluded middle, without there being any implication of defect of sanity on his part or lack of orderliness in the Reality he is trying to represent.

Actually it is not hard to see how the logical dichotomy falls short of being all embracing. Thus, the two classes of A and not-A, which are supposed to embrace all that is, actually do not embrace the thinker who is forming the classification. This is true even when the two classes consist of the Self and the not-Self. The Self in the classification is a projected Self, and therefore an object, and thus is not the actual cognizing witness. The latter embraces both classes, but is not contained privatively in either one. Therefore, it can lie only in the excluded middle.

4. The reality of God as the Supreme Value is not questioned here. The Supreme Value exists in the human soul and may be realized directly. It is the Other that completes the lonely self. The Supreme Value is the Presence in mystic realization. The error of many unphilosophical mystics lies in interpreting the Presence as an existence *in re*, that is, as an objective thing. In the true understanding of the real

nature of God, Meister Eckhart reveals himself as one of the clearest seeing of all mystics. For Eckhart, God is the other of the self, and these two stand in a relation of mutual dependence. Hence, God is not a nonrelative primal principle. This primal principle Eckhart called the God-head, a notion that is used by him in a sense analogous to the Buddhistic Shunyata.

5. That mystical insight is a source of knowledge is a primary thesis of the present work. The correctness of this thesis may be, and has been, challenged both on epistemological and psychological grounds. The justification of the thesis thus consists of two parts: (a) justification as against philosophic criticism; and (b) justification as against psychological criticism. The justification as against philosophical criticism is dealt with in various places throughout this work. The second justification is not needed on the level of Recognition itself, but only for the strictly relative type of consciousness.

6. See Section LX, "The Symbol of the Fourth Dimension," in *Pathways Through to Space*.

7. This alteration of the location of apparent activity is illustrated by the familiar experience of seemingly seeing surrounding objects move when one looks forth from a train that is starting to leave a station.

8. *The Secret Doctrine*, 3rd Ed., p. 67.

9. Quoted from Baldwin's *Dictionary of Philosophy and Psychology*, Vol. II, p. 614.

10. For an able discussion of Aestheticism as the predominant form of oriental philosophy, see F. S. C. Northrop's *The Meeting of East and West*.

11. See *The Life Divine* by Sri Aurobindo, Chapter IX, "The Pure Existent," p. 68.

12. The seeker or one who is practicing Yoga.

13. For an illuminating discussion of illusionism, see *The Life Divine* by Sri Aurobindo, Book II, Chapters V and VI.

14. *Critique of Pure Reason*. Max Muller translation, p. 293.

15. *Critique of Pure Reason*. Max Muller translation, pp. 217, 219. Italics mine.

Notes